Millay in Greenwich Village

Millay in

The University of Alabama

ANNE CHENEY

Greenwich Village

Press · *University, Alabama*

To my parents
Billie and Alan Cheney
and to the memory of
Dayton M. Kohler

Contents

Acknowledgments

Without much help and encouragement, I could not have completed this biography. I especially wish to thank Dr. Claude R. Flory, a gentleman, scholar, and friend; the other members of my committee, Dr. Fred Standley, Dr. James Preu, Dr. Mary Magginis, and Dr. John Boda; all those who granted me interviews; Mrs. Ben Carroll and Mrs. Ann Lo of Florida State University's Interlibrary Loan Division; Dr. Norman A. Brittin of Auburn University; Dean Thomas Gilmer of Virginia Polytechnic Institute and State University; Dr. Wilson C. Snipes, who made possible my leave of absence from Virginia Polytechnic Institute and State University; Prof. Sandra T. Long for her artwork; Mary Ann Brown and Ann Rutledge, my loyal friends; and, most of all, Warren.

Chronology

1892   Edna St. Vincent Millay is born in Rockland, Maine, on February 22 to Henry Tolman Millay and Cora Buzzelle Millay.

1900   Parents are divorced.

1901   Enjoys walking and swimming on the Maine seacoast,
to   where the experience of nearly drowning occurs that
1904   is later the subject of "Renascence."

1905   Attends high school in Camden, Maine. Spends free
to   time playing piano, reading, and writing poetry.
1909

1912   "Renascence" is published in *The Lyric Year*. Caroline Dow offers financial assistance for Millay's application to Vassar College. Witter Bynner and Arthur Davison Ficke write Millay on Thanksgiving Day.

1913   Millay first arrives in New York. Begins semester at Barnard College in February. Visits Armory Show and calls *Nude Descending a Staircase* a "pile of shingles" on March 8. First meets Witter Bynner on March 9. Begins four years at Vassar in September.

1914   Henry Noble MacCracken, who understood Millay's rebellious infractions of rules, becomes president of

Vassar in December.

1915 Attends Vassar. Is active in musical and dramatic per-
to   formances.
1916

1917 Graduates from Vassar with A. B. In fall, moves to
New York, where she first meets Floyd Dell at audition of *The Angel Intrudes*, Eugen Boissevain—to
their mutual indifference—and Harrison Dowd.

1918 Edna and Norma Millay move to Greenwich Village in
January. Millay writes "Memorial to D. C." after
death of Dorothy Coleman, a Vassar classmate. First
meets John Reed, Allan Ross Macdougall, W.
Adolphe Roberts, and Arthur Davison Ficke, her
"spiritual advisor." Attends both *Masses'* trials with
Dell in April and October. Begins publishing in
Ainslee's.

1919 Writes "Lord Archer, Death" to John Reed. First
performance of *Aria da Capo* on December 5. Arthur
D. Ficke meets Gladys Brown, thus ending his serious
interest in Millay.

1920 First meets Edmund Wilson and Frank Crowninshield. Begins publishing in *Vanity Fair*. Sacco and
Vanzetti are arrested for murder on April 15.

1921 Makes trip to Europe. Writes in a letter to Ficke, "We
shall never escape from each other." Makes tentative
plans to marry Witter Bynner. Writes *The Lamp and
the Bell.*

1922 Continues European travel.

1923 Returns to New York. Meets Eugen Boissevain for
second time. Marries Boissevain in Croton-on-Hudson
on July 18. Reads sonnet "The Pioneer" dedicated to
Inez Milholland to National Women's Party in Washington, D. C., on November 18.

1924 Moves with Boissevain to "dollhouse" at 75½ Bedford Street, a few blocks from Chumley's Bar.

1925   End of Millay's Village days. Millay and Boissevain move to Steepletop in Austerlitz, New York, in summer.

1926   Visits Fickes in Santa Fe, New Mexico.

1927   Millay and John Dos Passos are arrested for participation in Sacco-Vanzetti protests. Boissevain bails them out on August 22. Sacco and Vanzetti are executed on August 23.

1928
to
1939   Lives at Steepletop. Health deteriorates.

1940   Feels deep concern over World War II. *Make Bright the Arrows* is published and harms Millay's reputation as a poet.

1941
to
1948   Becomes increasingly reclusive at Steepletop and Ragged Island. Returns to nature poetry, which was not fully appreciated until after her death. Has nervous breakdown in 1944 and does not write for two years.

1949   Eugen Boissevain dies of stroke on August 30. Millay is deeply grieved.

1950   Millay dies of heart attack on October 18.

Millay in Greenwich Village

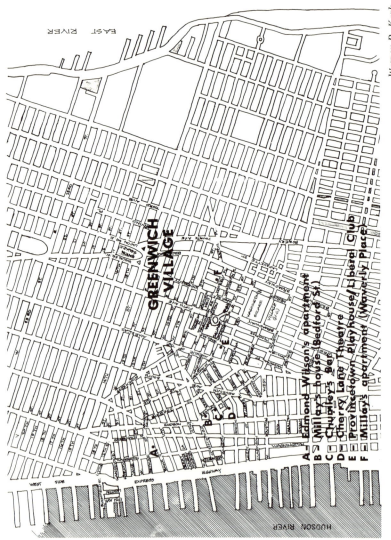

GREENWICH VILLAGE

A — Edmund Wilson's apartment
B — Millay's house (Bedford St.)
C — Chumley's Bar
D — Cherry Lane Theatre
E — Provincetown Playhouse/Liberal Club
F — Millay's apartment (Waverly Place)

EAST RIVER

HUDSON RIVER

WEST SIDE EXPRESS HIGHWAY

Warren R. Kark

Introduction

My candle burns at both ends;
  It will not last the night;
But ah, my foes, and oh, my friends—
  It gives a lovely light!

This quatrain, now embedded in the American consciousness, provides a glimpse into the colorful, rebellious personality of one of the most important poets of the twentieth century— Edna St. Vincent Millay. We can almost envision the slender young woman reciting the poem, her green eyes sparkling and her long auburn hair quietly swishing. Edna Millay captured the freedom, spontaneity, quick wit, and beauty of the Pre-Twenties (1910-20) as no other poet did. She served as a living symbol of women who could live, think, and love as freely as they chose.

Scattered throughout Millay's life were an array of lovers, series of all-night parties in the Village and on the Left Bank, brief stays in jail for political protest, involvements in women's rights movements, moments of ecstasy at Beethoven concerts. But Millay also had her "nunlike" side. She spent endless hours, days, years searching for the perfect word to complete a poem; she suffered headaches and general poor

health. As a young woman, she maintained love for an unre-
sponsive suitor for years; she quietly played her grand piano
in troubled times. Exclaiming "What should I be but a harlot
and a nun? / What should I be but a prophet and a liar?,"
Millay hinted at the multiplicity of her personality.

To explore the complex personality and works of Edna St.
Vincent Millay, I have chosen to write a psychological biography, hoping to catch the nuances of her essence. Frequently I
have been forced to depart from strict chronological order,
for psychological time is more important. Yet I have tried to
keep the illusion firmly rooted in reality by using Karl Yost's
extremely reliable *A Bibliography of the Works of Edna St.
Vincent Millay* (1936) to determine the actual dates when
Millay composed specific Village poems.

A highly personal poet, Edna St. Vincent Millay has been
called "not an intellect but a sensibility" by Allen Tate—a
valid and positive criticism. Millay was at her best when
writing about the emotions, especially in her love sonnets,
yet she always maintained intellectual control of her subject.
Her fine balance of the emotional and the intellectual, her
"capacity for ecstacy...in its true Greek sense of standing outside the self," her conviction that women should be free to
love and feel deeply are best exhibited in sonnets written
during her Village days.

Psychological time is especially appropriate in treating Millay's love affairs. Alexander McKaig, a close friend of
Edmund (Bunny) Wilson, suggests the complexity of Millay's
relationships with men in this diary entry: "Modern Sappho.
18 love affairs and now Bunny is thinking of marrying her."
Even a treatment of the most important men in her life—
Floyd Dell, Edmund Wilson, Arthur Davison Ficke, and
Eugen Boissevain—defies neat chronological ordering. Based
on the dates when Millay first met each man, the order of her
suitors would be: Floyd Dell, Eugen Boissevain, Arthur Davison Ficke, and Edmund Wilson. But this order becomes con-

fused for two reasons: (1) Millay corresponded with Ficke for six years before she met him in 1918, during which time she viewed him as her "spiritual advisor," and although Millay's first meeting with Ficke was highly romantic, she did not seem to realize his full impact until 1921 or later; and, (2) her first reaction to Eugen Boissevain in 1917 was apathetic, but their whirlwind courtship in 1923 culminated in marriage. Therefore, psychological time is a more appropriate means of ordering Millay's suitors than chronological time, with the final order becoming: Dell, Wilson, Ficke, and Boissevain. As for the other "18 love affairs," the influence of these men on Millay is interesting but minor; they did not influence substantially the progression of her view of love from transience to permanence. I have, therefore, included them in a separate chapter.

As a psychological biography, *Millay in Greenwich Village* deals with Millay's initiation into maturity as a person and an artist in the Village. Just as in a religious ritual of initiation we must recognize the inexperience and naivité of the novice or neophyte before the ceremony to fully perceive his or her newfound insight and maturity afterwards, we must envision Millay as a novice—as a child in Camden, Maine, as a young woman in Poughkeepsie, New York—to understand her metamorphosis in Greenwich Village. Therefore, in Chapter One, "A Sense of Glad Awakening," I have outlined carefully her early views of religion and sex, which were to change radically in the Village.

Although as a young girl in Camden, Maine, Edna Millay was a member of the Congregational Church, the Christian convictions resounding through "Renascence," which she first conceived when she was no more than ten years old and wrote when she was eighteen, reflect an almost pantheistic love of nature, God, and man. But Millay supplanted this joyful love with dour, guilt-ridden puritanism in "The Interim" and "The Suicide." Thus, Millay needed her "teachers" in the

Village—the street people and perhaps the paintings of John Sloan—to give her the new insight to express her all-embracing love of mankind in "Macdougal Street" and "Recuerdo."

Even more dramatic than her change in religious attitudes was Millay's sexual metamorphosis. While at Vassar, she found more meaning in friendships with women than with men, and her play *The Lamp and the Bell* and her poem "Memorial to D.C." celebrate the power of lesbian love. Again, she needed her "teachers," Floyd Dell and other lovers, to initiate her into heterosexual love, which she so deftly expressed in sonnets such as "What lips my lips have kissed," "Into the golden vessel of great song," and "Love is not all."

Not only did Millay's friends in the Village serve as teachers, but Greenwich Village itself served as the catalyst in and the scene of important transformations in Millay's life and works. Since Edgar Allan Poe's time, the Village has served as a mecca for artists and writers where they could confront the essential facts of life and enjoy maximum individual freedom. Here Millay was exposed to the most avant-garde ideas of the day, developed a broader concept of religion, and shifted from lesbian to heterosexual love. On the narrow twisting streets, in the little delicatessens, in intimate bars and restaurants embedded in tiny spaces, lovers could freely hold hands or embrace, they could sing aloud or speak to strangers—they were free of the repressions and limitations of the Silent Majority.

Friends and scholars of Millay argue vehemently about the actual influence Greenwich Village had on Millay. Jean Morris Pettit feels that the devil-may-care attitude of Millay's writing has been overplayed and unfairly so and further that the Millay Legend is founded upon small fact and much fiction. Both Witter Bynner and Floyd Dell wrote Norman Brittin that Millay would have been essentially the same person if she had never lived in the Village. Yet Malcolm Cowley and others feel that the Village was a significant factor in Millay's life and works.

Although Millay's life in the Village was the source of her finest work, several critics have tended to dismiss it as serious work, perhaps in resentment over the immense popularity Millay has enjoyed. Hildegarde Flanner dismisses Millay's Village poetry as petty and slight. Louise Bogan comments that a certain hampering nihilism prevented Millay from breaking through to impressive maturity. What they fail to acknowledge, however, is the careful craftsmanship and avant-garde thought of such sonnets as "Into the golden vessel of great song," "And you as well must die, beloved dust," and "Only until this cigarette is ended."

Due to the influence of her "lovers and thinkers" and the general atmosphere of freedom and exploration in the Village, Millay crystallized many ideas and attitudes that freed her to write her five best volumes of poetry—*Renascence and Other Poems* (1917), *A Few Figs from Thistles* (1920), *The Harp-Weaver and Other Poems* (1923), and *The Buck in the Snow and Other Poems* (1928). Despite some of her friends' opinions to the contrary, Millay could never have written these poems in Camden, Maine, or Poughkeepsie, New York; for in the Village, Millay found much of what Lambert Strether found in Paris—the courage to live spontaneously, to love deeply, to feel grief and loneliness unashamedly, to find beauty and meaning in culture, to defy death. *Millay in Greenwich Village* is not a comprehensive biography; that has already been written by Norman Brittin and Miriam Gurko. Instead, I have written a psychological portrait of Millay at her finest, after the repressions of her childhood and youth and before the stifling bonds of her marriage. Only in the Village could Millay have expressed the beauty and pain of fleeting love:

What lips my lips have kissed, and where, and why,
I have forgotten, and what arms have lain
Under my head til morning; but the rain
Is full of ghosts tonight, that tap and sigh
Upon the glass and listen for reply,
And in my heart there stirs a quiet pain
For unremembered lads that not again
Will turn to me at midnight with a cry.
Thus in the winter stands the lonely tree,
Nor knows what birds have vanished one by one,
Yet knows its boughs more silent than before:
I cannot say what loves have come and gone,
I only know that summer sang in me
A little while, that in me sings no more.

1

A SENSE OF
GLAD AWAKENING:

Millay's Childhood and Youth

God, Death, and Youth—Millay's Childhood

One summer afternoon, a short, slender, auburn-haired girl stood on an unfamiliar beach and peered across the Maine sea. An emerald island beckoned far away. Excited by the challenge, she dived in and swam evenly but deliberately, tiring as she approached her goal. As she reached for the edge of the island, it slipped between her fingers; the island was a mass of floating seaweed. Struggling for breath and expelling mouthfuls of salt water, she tried to remain calm. Fatigue began to overcome her, but she thrust her way to the beach with slow, rapid, then slow strokes. When she reached the shore, she collapsed with relief. Edna St. Vincent Millay had had a narrow brush with death.[1]

As a child, Millay enjoyed wandering on the rough and jagged Maine beach, strewn with driftwood and dotted with seagulls. Away from the happy chaos of home, she had time to ponder about her life and to enjoy the mere fact of being alive—a feeling shared by almost anyone who has trudged a deserted winter beach alone. Mulling over her near drowning at no more than ten years old, at eighteen (in 1910) she wrote "Renascence," which in many ways is the record of her spiritual growth during adolescence.

The narrator in "Renascence," as she stares out at the distant island, wonders if she will ever escape the confinement and boredom of her home:

> All I could see from where I stood
> Was three long mountains and a wood;
> I turned and looked another way,
> And saw three islands in a bay.

As the sky seems to close in on her, she perhaps wishes for a spiritual death:

> The sky, I thought, is not so grand;
> I 'most could touch it with my hand!
> And reaching up my hand to try,
> I screamed, to feel it touch the sky.

She then dives into the water for the difficult swim.

Discovering that the island is only seaweed, gasping for air, experiencing a symbolic spiritual death, she imagines herself beneath the earth, where she attains an almost Christ-like knowledge, similar to that of the crucifixion:

> All sin was of my sinning, all
> Atoning mine, and mine the gall
> Of all regret. Mine was the weight
> Of every brooded wrong, the hate
> That stood behind each envious thrust,
> Mine every greed, mine every lust.

In the cool earth, she feels the suffering of all men, a man starving in Capri, two ships sinking. But death is not the answer:

> Yet lay the weight so close about
> There was no room for it without.
> And so beneath the weight lay I
> And suffered death, but could not die.

She reaches the shore only with great difficulty. As she flings herself upon the beach, she feels "a sense of glad awakening" similar to Christian rebirth:

> O God, I cried, give me new birth,
> And put me back upon the earth!

Feeling a profound sense of joy in earthly beauty, she winds her arms around trees and hugs the ground. Lying exhausted on the beach, she sees not only beauty, but danger, in the emerald island. With new, almost pantheistic knowledge of God, the narrator concludes with a reaffirmation of exultant joy in earthly beauty:[2]

> The world stands out on either side
> No wider than the heart is wide;
> Above the world is stretched the sky,—
> No higher than the soul is high.
> The heart can push the sea and land
> Farther away on either hand;
> The soul can split the sky in two,
> And let the face of God shine through.
> But East and West will pinch the heart
> That can not keep them pushed apart;
> And he whose soul is flat—the sky
> Will cave in on him by and by.

Two years later, in 1912, "Renascence" fulfilled its own prophesy of releasing Millay from her earth-bound prison when the poem placed fourth in Ferdinand Earle's national contest *The Lyric Year*. When Caroline Dow heard Millay read "Renascence" later that year, she was so impressed by the poet's beauty, intelligence, and talent that she offered her a four-year scholarship to Vassar College. Freed by these events from "the things that bounded me," Millay had an even greater sense of glad awakening.

In 1910 Millay had written two other poems dealing with death and Christianity, "Interim" and "The Suicide," but they contain elements of guilt and puritanism. Not her finest poems, even Witter Bynner, later to become one of her lovers and thinkers in the Village, felt that they are "long, rather callow poems." (At about the same time, Millay also wrote "God's World," a simple, but moving, statement of pantheism, and two other poems that flippantly defy death, "The

Shroud" and "If I should learn, in some quite casual way.")
Certainly "Interim" and "The Suicide" do not reflect the
intense personal experience and keen enjoyment of life of
"Renascence," but they are important in illustrating Millay's
predominant concept of Christianity prior to the Village.

Despite some simple, though effective, imagery, "Interim"
is basically an unrelieved complaint against the sudden death
of the narrator's sweetheart. Recalling her small frame, her
eccentric, bold handwriting, the male narrator captures the
essence of his childlike lover through simple details—her book
facedown on the table, the chair pushed away from the table,
her last written words, "I picked the first sweet-pea today."
Unfortunately, the second half of "Interim" degenerates into
random and commonplace Christian observations—"Am I
gone mad / That I should spit upon a rosary?" and "Not
truth, but faith, it is / That keeps the world alive"—
interspersed with invocations to an ineffectual God "God!—
God pity me!" With no suggestion of the Christian rebirth of
"Renascence," the narrator concludes "Interim" with no
clear philosophical resolution:

> Ah, I am worn out—I am wearied out—
> It is too much—I am but flesh and blood,
> And I must sleep. Though you were dead again,
> I am but flesh and blood and I must sleep.

Perhaps "Interim" fails to reach the heights of "Renascence" because Millay chose the masculine point of view—a
nearly impossible task for a poet so intensely personal and
feminine. More significantly, Millay did not have a serious
suitor, much less a lover, in Camden. Instead, she preferred
the company of her sisters and other girls, particularly members of the Genethood, a club organized by the Congregational Church. She even harbored an active dislike for Henry
Hall, who defeated her for class poet in 1909; the girls voted
for Millay, but the boys voted for Hall because Millay offered
them too much intellectual competition.[3]

In "The Suicide," the narrator kills herself to escape a feeling of confinement, of boredom:

> I asked of thee no favour save this one:
> That thou wouldst leave me playing in the sun!
> And this thou didst deny....

After her death, she ascends to a literal heaven, where she plays the harp, which eventually becomes boring. When she asks a kind, but mirthless God for other tasks, he replies, "Thou hadst thy task, and laidst it by...." Neither "Interim" nor "The Suicide" offer any possibility for new life and insight.

Millay's adolescent fear of death and concern with the repressions of Christianity well may have stemmed from attitudes formed in her childhood. Cora Millay and her three daughters—Edna, Norma, and Kathleen—were noted in Camden, Maine, for their unconventional attitudes and behavior, yet the Millays cherished a deep love for each other and had an awareness of Christian doctrine. They frequently attended the Elm Street Congregational Church in Camden, where Millay formed a close friendship with her Sunday School teacher, Abbie Huston Evans, herself a poet who published in national magazines. By the age of twelve, Millay had read most of the poems of John Milton. Perhaps Millay recalled the fallen angels and the literal hell of *Paradise Lost* when she wrote "Interim" and "The Suicide."

Just as Millay hugged the ground and embraced the trees in "Renascence," she celebrated the winds, skies, and mists with childlike fervor in "God's World":

> O World, I cannot hold thee close enough!
>   Thy winds, thy wide grey skies!
>   Thy mists, that roll and rise!
> Thy woods, this autumn day, that ache and sag
> And all but cry with colour! That gaunt crag
> To crush! To lift the lean of that black bluff!
> World, World, I cannot get thee close enough!

> Long have I known a glory in it all,
>   But never knew I this:
>   Here such a passion is
> As stretcheth me apart,—Lord, I do fear
> Thou'st made the world too beautiful this year;
> My soul is all but out of me,—let fall
> No burning leaf; prithee, let no bird call.

She strongly suggests the idea of pantheism in the line, "My soul is all but out of me...," just as Emerson thought the "oversoul," in which man, nature, and God are inseparably intertwined, was the universal soul of all living things.

Despite her meditations on death and God, Millay never lost her spontaneous sense of humor. Once in high school someone told her that if she stole apples, she would get a stomach-ache. She promptly climbed a tree, stole some apples, ate them, and declared that they were the most delicious apples she had ever eaten.

Never accepting conventional norms or attitudes, Millay gradually began to lose her fear of death and belief in the repressive tenets of Christianity. In both "The Shroud" and "If I should learn, in some quite casual way," Millay inserts a note of flippancy that later dominates her Village poetry. At first she treats death with mock reverence in "The Shroud," but then she laughs at its very presence:

> Death, I say, my heart is bowed
>   Unto thine,—O mother!
> This red gown will make a shroud
>   Good as any other!

Combining pseudosophistication and controlled grief in "If I should learn, in some quite casual way," the narrator imagines that as she rides the subway, she reads in the newspaper that her lover has been killed:

> I should not cry aloud—I could not cry
> Aloud, or wring my hands in such a place—
> I should but watch the station lights rush by

> With a more careful interest on my face;
> Or raise my eyes and read with greater care
> Where to store furs and how to treat the hair.

Even before entering Vassar, Millay was beginning to believe that death was not necessarily a matter of Christianity and was to be thwarted with physical resistance.

Millay's friends disagree about the extent of her Christianity. Gladys Brown Ficke, the widow of Arthur Davison Ficke, declared that Millay was not a "female Jesus" and that "She could be a bitch on occasion...."[4] Apparently Mrs. Ficke feared that treating Millay within a Christian context would reduce the poet's rebellious and spontaneous nature to that of saccharine submission—an unfounded fear. Vincent Sheean, who interviewed Millay late in her life, thinks that all of Millay's poetry was influenced by her strong Christianity. But Edmund Wilson, one of her Village associates and a lifelong friend, is the most correct when he says in *The Shores of Light* that God did not appear in her work after the early poems "God's World" and "Renascence."

Discarding her fear of death and belief in the more repressive elements of Christianity, Millay found solace in pantheism and the beauty of man and nature during her Village days. But earthly beauty is sadly fleeting, as Millay later noted in "Dirge Without Music":

> The answers quick and keen, the honest look, the
>   laughter, the love,—
> They are gone. They are gone to feed the roses.
>   Elegant and curled
> Is the blossom. Fragrant is the blossom. I know. But I
>   do not approve.
> More precious was the light in your eyes than all the
>   roses in the world.
>
> Down, down, down into the darkness of the grave
> Gently they go, the beautiful, the tender, the kind;
> Quietly they go, the intelligent, the witty, the brave.
> I know. But I do not approve. And I am not resigned.

The Lamp and the Bell—*Vassar*

On the small island of Lesbos, lush with roses, violets, and grapes yielding excellent wine, lived the small, dark-haired poet Sappho in the sixth century B.C. Establishing herself at an early age as a poet and woman of brilliance, she gathered about her young girls of the upper classes, whom she taught poetry, music, and dancing. She referred to these young girls as her *hetaerae,* or "intimate companions." Though she was fond of most of her students, she was especially drawn to Atthis, Telesippa, and Megara. When Sappho discovered that Atthis favored Andromeda, a woman who directed an academy, above herself, she invoked the goddess of love:

> Shimmering-throned immortal Aphrodite,
> Daughter of Zeus, Enchantress, I implore thee,
> Spare me, O Queen, this agony and anguish,
> Crush not my spirit.[5]

When Atthis died at an early age, Sappho was grief stricken.

When Sappho was in her fifties, she fell in love with the perhaps mythological Phaon, a boatsman so handsome that some said that Aphrodite had given him a magic ointment that made him irresistible to women. Without telling Sappho, Phaon one day left Lesbos. In despair, Sappho flung herself from the Leudacian Cliff, a white stone that rises sheer out of the dark sea below.

Millay admired Sappho greatly. In her living room at Steepletop, where she lived from 1925 to 1950, Millay kept a bronze bust of Sappho on a marble pedestal. Sappho probably influenced Millay's poetry; the line from "Renascence," "I screamed to feel it touch the sky," closely resembles Sappho's "I do not think to touch the sky with my two arms." Several of Millay's poems pertain to Sappho, including "Sappho Crosses the Dark River into Hades" and "Evening on Lesbos." Also, both women wrote of love, Sappho being closer to Millay in frankness and sensuality than more contemporary women poets such as Emily Dickinson, Sara Teas-

dale, and Elinor Wylie. Finally, Millay perhaps learned from
Sappho the concept of *agape*, particularly as it pertains to
deep friendships between women. (*Agape* is a totally selfless,
deeply spiritual love. A higher form of more physical love, or
philos, agape is other-directed, almost divine love). Lesbian
agape is the controlling theme of both *The Lamp and the Bell*
and "Memorial to D. C."

Just as Sappho surrounded herself with young girls, at Vassar (1913-17) Millay gathered about her a circle of close
friends—Charlotte (Charlie) Babcock, Anne Gardner, Frances
Stout, Isobel Simpson, and Dorothy Coleman. Millay held
Charlie, a pretty, plump, blue-eyed young woman, dearest of
her Vassar group, as she revealed by her reaction to her "dear
sister's" impending marriage to Mac Sills after graduating
from Vassar in 1917. Characteristically, Millay treated the
marriage in an outwardly lighthearted fashion, but in several
unpublished letters she could not mask her profound sense of
loss: "Charlie, I love you very dearly. Don't forget me
entirely, just on account of that Mac Sills,—will you?" Three
months later, Millay wrote Charlie, "Yes, dear, I will come
and visit you if Mac goes away, and if you still want me."[6]
At Vassar, Millay dreaded the transient nature of love
between women even more than she regretted passing loves
with men.

Although Millay's love for Isobel Simpson and Anne Gardner was less intense than that for Charlie, it was real nevertheless. Her love for Isobel Simpson was both idyllic and spontaneous. Once Millay wrote Isobel, "Someday I shall write a
great poem to you," and later she teasingly wrote "that little
sphinx" that when she saw her again she wanted to hear her
"squeak such a silly little squeak." The tone of her letter to
Anne Gardner is remarkably similar to a letter she wrote to
Arthur Davison Ficke, a highly romantic figure in her life:
"Ours was a perfect friendship....And it doesn't matter if we
never write, and never see each other, it is just the same...."

Millay's lesbianism possibly could be traced to her family background. Due to her mother's divorce from her father in 1900 when Millay was only eight years old, perhaps Millay suffered from the lack of a strong father figure and drew strength from the close, uninhibited love of her mother and sisters. But Cora and Henry Millay had parted with a minimum of bitterness, and Henry, despite his gambling and drinking, retained a deep affection for his daughters, as is indicated by his gifts of money and sporadic visits. A more accurate explanation may be that Millay found in women a chance for a more equal, truly reciprocal love.

Two modern treatments of lesbianism—*The Group* by Mary McCarthy and *The Fox* by D. H. Lawrence—parallel the deeper reasons for Millay's sapphic tendencies. The members of the Group, eight young Vassar women who form the Daisy Chain, maintain love for each other regardless of what men pass in and out of their lives. Lakey, in particular, resembles Millay in that she is the leader of the Group—the most creative and most independent. (Mary McCarthy denies that Lakey is modeled on Millay,[7] but McCarthy certainly had access to extensive personal knowledge since both McCarthy and Millay had intense relationships with Edmund Wilson.) In *The Fox,* the two women assume traditional male and female roles—March chops wood and hunts, while Banford cooks, sews, and nurtures her lover's ego—but they share an intense affection that is not matched by the man who eventually intervenes and destroys their idyllic life. Perhaps Millay felt that women understood each other better than they understood men because the similarity of their psychological makeup and bodies led to a sensitive, truly reciprocal love. She also found pleasure in the purely physical aspect of lesbian lovemaking, according to two reliable sources who prefer to remain anonymous.

Not only did the Millay coterie at Vassar share deep love for one another, they also enjoyed a spectrum of highly creative and spontaneous activities. Shortly after entering Vassar in 1913, Millay wrote "Oh, the daisy-chain marshal wears a rose and gray dress / That cost a million dollars, not a cent more or less! / (The Post inserts this item as it gallops to press)." The Daisy Chain was but one of the many traditions and activities that she shared with her Vassar friends. (The Daisy Chain and the Daisy Parade were parts of the ceremony in which the sophomores honored the Vassar seniors.) Noted for singing, constant theatrical performances, and academic excellence, Vassar served as an effective catalyst to refine Millay's creative abilities.

Millay had her difficulties adjusting to Vassar. Entering Vassar when she was twenty-one, she was about four years older than the average freshman. She found many of the rules ridiculous and rebelled by smoking (smoking was banned) at the nearby cemetery, frequently cutting classes, and explaining her absence from chapel with excuses such as "It was raining and I was afraid the red on the pew would fade on my new dress." She was, however, a brilliant student in languages and literature, though she did not fare so well in history and mathematics. While Millay's intimate group was devoted to her, some students and professors were offended by her cavalier attitude.

In 1917 Millay had an opportunity to hear Caruso sing *Aida* in New York. Unfortunately, the performance was scheduled for two days after classes began at Vassar. Undaunted, Millay heard Caruso and was subsequently "campused." After two months of good behavior, she yielded to the temptation to take a long ride with Charlie Babcock and two other friends. After spending the night with a friend's parents, they had coffee the next morning at an inn, where Millay signed the guest book. A few days later, a Vassar warden spotted the signature and reported Millay's violation. Although the faculty voted to suspend Millay indefinitely, Dr. MacCracken, the president, vetoed the suspension since she was on the verge of graduation. Millay had already missed the baccalaurate sermon, but she attended commencement. She wrote her mother, "Commencement went off beautifully...Vincent (Edna St. Vincent Millay A.B.!)."

Three years earlier (1914), at the beginning of Millay's sophomore year, the youthful Henry Noble MacCracken had become the new president of Vassar; he later recounted his experiences there in *The Hickory Limb*. He was a protégé of George Lyman Kittredge, progressive, and sympathetic toward his students. Although deeply interested in women's suffrage, MacCracken was still prey to feminine wiles: "Vassar tears flowed like a river. I sat silent and miserable while student or teacher wept on." At times he exhibited a sense of affected naiveté, which, combined with his subtle sense of humor, no doubt endeared him to many of his students, including Millay. Once when asked about the status of the sex problem at Vassar, he replied: "Knowing nothing about sex whatever except what I read in Chaucer, I haven't much to say."[8] MacCracken often supported Millay by winking at her many infractions of rules, while some other professors were impatient with her blasé attitude. MacCracken well may have enhanced Millay's awareness of a strong male figure, a concept that eventually led to her conversion from lesbianism to heterosexuality.

While at Vassar, Millay's basic ideas continued to shift from a tendency toward provincialism to a more cosmopolitan outlook. In 1915 Inez Milholland, a lawyer and suffragette, visited Vassar, and, according to MacCracken, "was the darling of the undergraduates." Inez, who was the first wife of Eugen Boissevain, later to be Millay's husband, rode a white horse at the head of the Suffrage Parade on Fifth Avenue. In 1923, Millay wrote a sonnet, "Upon this marble bust that is not I," which she later dedicated to Inez Milholland.

Drama had always been one of Millay's serious interests. In a play-writing course at Vassar she wrote three plays, *The*

Princess Marries the Page, Two Slatterns and a King, and *The Wall of Dominoes.* After graduation she wrote three more plays, *Aria da Capo, The King's Henchman,* and *The Lamp and the Bell. Aria da Capo,* generally considered to be Millay's best play, is an incisive satire on war and man's basic greed. Lacking the initial impact of *Aria da Capo, The Lamp and the Bell* is often dismissed as obviously having been written for the Vassar theater and as being somewhat melodramatic. Despite its dependence on a rapid succession of more than twenty scenes, a cast of over sixty characters, and period costumes, the play is notable, nevertheless, for its quiet, but powerful, celebration of selfless love between women.

Even though Millay wrote *The Lamp and the Bell* in Paris in 1921, the spirit of the play clearly comes from her days at Vassar. At the core of the play is the unselfish love between the more masculine, intelligent princess, Beatrice, and the more feminine, fragile daughter of Queen Octavia, Bianca. With the exception of Beatrice and Bianca, most of the characters in *The Lamp and the Bell* are stereotypes. Octavia, King Lorenzo's second wife, is the mildly wicked queen, perhaps a fastidious dean of women. The practical, humorous, and compassionate Lorenzo, who adores his daughter, is highly reminiscent of MacCracken.

Lorenzo is the most believable male character. Fidelio, the jester, is likeable and wise, but somewhat effeminate. (He resembles a Shakespearian wise fool.) Guido, the illegitimate nephew of Lorenzo, is a pasteboard villain.[9] Guido tries to destroy Beatrice because she has spurned him and failed to recognize that

> I am a man. You should have thought
> Of that before.

He is jealous also of her superior horsemanship and of the deep respect she elicits from servants and commoners. But the stereotypes of *The Lamp and the Bell* do not detract from the play as a whole. Millay creates a rich tapestry of basically feminine emotions and situations in which there are vignettes of unrequited love, jealousy, power struggles, and romantic triangles.

Just as *The Lamp and the Bell* is based on Millay's Vassar days, Beatrice and Bianca well may be modeled on Millay herself and Charlotte Babcock. Throughout the play, Beatrice seems more masculine, whereas Bianca is softer and more feminine. Laura, the maid, says,

> I vow I never knew a pair of lovers
> More constant than those two.

After Beatrice and Bianca have known each other for four years, Bianca remarks,

> I still, though,
> Think of you as a Princess: the way you do things
> Is much more wonderful than the way I do them!—

Bianca then asks who will be married first and if their friendship will endure. Beatrice is supportive and comforting:

> Oh, you are tired, tired, you are very tired.
> You must be rocked to sleep, and tucked in bed,
> And have your eyelids kissed to make you dream
> Of fairies!

Octavia decides "Tis not good two young girls / To be so much together" and sends Bianca away for six months. While Bianca is absent, Beatrice and Mario, King of Lagoverde, fall in love. When Bianca returns, Mario falls in love with Bianca because "Her gentleness has crept so / Into my heart...." Beatrice is deeply hurt by Mario's change of affections, but in order to protect Bianca she does not tell her friend of her relationship with Mario.

The central scene of *The Lamp and the Bell,* concerning Beatrice's sense of loss over Bianca's impending marriage, is very similar to Millay's sorrow over Charlie's marriage to Mac Sills. The entire scene between the two young women on Bianca's wedding day is fraught with irony. Yearning for Beatrice's approval, Bianca says,

> I could not bear
> To wed a man that was displeasing to you.

A few days before Charlie's wedding in 1917, Millay wrote her "dear sister," "You know how beautiful I want it all to be for you and Mac, I think.—I wish I might be there Thursday—you will be so lovely to see...." In the play, Beatrice almost breaks through her facade of lightheartedness when she tells Bianca, "You do not know, maybe, how much I love you." Millay's letter to Charlie reflects the same playfulness, laced with regret, as she enclosed a bit of doggerel with the gift of a teaball:

> When you think of me,
> Blow in a cup, and make some tea!
> Rotten bad form although it be,
> Blow in a cup, and make some tea.
> This kind of tea ball—open wide—
> Will not become mildewed inside.
> And when you use it—think of me,
> Blow in a cup and make some tea!

One year later, Millay wrote her friend, "I really care—and love you very much."[10]

At the end of the scene in *The Lamp and the Bell,* the impending wedding is temporarily forgotten as each girl declares her love for the other. Bianca vows,

> You are a burning lamp to me, a flame
> The wind cannot blow out, and I shall hold you
> High in my hand against whatever darkness.

Beatrice responds,

> You are to me a silver bell in a tower.
> And when it rings I know I am near home.

The image that each young woman uses is related to her personality. Bianca's image is distinctly more feminine; the lamp is a symbol of warmth and security "against whatever darkness." The flame also is an emblem of passion, but the passion may be ephemeral; there is the threat that the wind will extinguish it. The bell, on the other hand, is a more substantial object; it is silver, metallic. Also, the bell is securely fixed in a tower. The lamp, then, signifies Bianca's need to be protected by Beatrice, while the bell typifies Beatrice's more rational love for Bianca. "When it rings I know I am near home" is suggestive of a hunter returning home at sunset; he is guided by, but not dependent upon, the bell.

Even the central symbols of the lamp and bell reflect the relationship between Edna Millay and Charlie Babcock. In an unpublished letter to Charlie in 1920, Millay wrote, "Good luck to you darling, and not *too* much discomfort, and a cute, pretty, ind o' fat, li'l' blue-eyed daughter, in every respect exactly like yourself, and oh, so much love from me!" Millay's tone here is encouraging and supportive. The mere fact of Charlie's pregnancy reflects her warmth and feminity. Although Millay later married, she did not have children.

Throughout the rest of *The Lamp and the Bell*, the love of Beatrice and Bianca is intertwined with their love for Mario. Perhaps Millay makes a comment on the relative strengths of feminine love and the love of a man and a woman. The night of Bianca's and Mario's wedding, Lorenzo dies, leaving Beatrice the queen of Fiori but grieved over her father's death. Thus, Bianca leaves Mario on their wedding night to comfort Beatrice. Bianca tells Mario,

> You know,
> How much I love you. But I could not be happy
> Thinking of her awake in the darkness, weeping, and all alone.

The friendship of Bianca and Beatrice is jeopardized five years later. Beatrice is riding in the woods one day when Guido, who is trying to usurp her power, sends his men to try to kill her. In the confusion of the scuffle, Beatrice draws her sword and kills Mario. No one knows that Beatrice has killed Mario except Anselmo, who is loyal to his mistress. When

Bianca visits her, however, Beatrice tells her the truth. Bianca leaves, uttering "God have mercy" as Beatrice falls unconscious.

Two years later, when Bianca is dying, she calls for Beatrice, who has just been overthrown by Guido. He allows Beatrice to leave prison to see Bianca only after he has extracted a promise from her:

> That upon returning
> You come to me, and give yourself to me,
> To lie in my arms lovingly.

Beatrice decides that "this foolish body" is less important than seeing Bianca and is released. Beatrice leaps to Bianca's bed as Bianca throws her arms around Beatrice's neck and dies. After her death, Bianca's maid conveys a message to Beatrice, "All is well, 'twixt her and you." The love of Beatrice and Bianca is reaffirmed as Beatrice declares,

> She is returned
> From long silence, and rings out above me
> Like a silver bell!—Let us go back, Fidelio,
> And gather up the fallen stones, and build us
> Another tower.

The love of Bianca and Beatrice seems to overpower either woman's love for Mario. Beatrice relinquishes Mario to Bianca in unselfish silence. After Beatrice kills Mario, the two women are silent for two years, but their reunion is a strong recapitulation of their earlier love for each other.

Just as Bianca and Beatrice are estranged by the death of Mario, Charlie Babcock was deeply wounded in 1941 by Millay's volume of war poetry *Make Bright the Arrows.* Charlie felt that this book of verse, in which Millay advocated America's entrance into World War II, indirectly might lead to the death of her sons. Millay poignantly explained the difference in their commitment to the national cause: "And though I have no sons to be caught in this war, if we are caught in it, I have one thing to give in the service of my country,–my reputation as a poet."[11] As the tower stood, so the flame wavered.

Thus, *The Lamp and the Bell* is a strong expression of unselfish love between women. Through the Beatrice-Bianca-Mario triangle, Millay implies that lesbian love is more powerful than heterosexual love, just as Millay grieved over the loss of Charlie to a husband and lamented their rift over the possible threat that *Make Bright the Arrows* held for Charlie's sons. Furthermore, Millay implies that intelligent women are adored by fathers, respected by inferiors, and resented by male peers. She saw marriage as more a concern of maternity than of romantic love. Finally, love between women, though it might be transient, is more noble than heterosexual love:

> This foolish body,
> That is not I! There is not I
> Saving the need I have to go to her!

Deeply grieved by the death of one of her close friends, in 1920 Millay wrote "Memorial to D. C."–still another treatment of love between women. When Dorothy Coleman, a native of Milwaukee, Wisconsin, entered Vassar College in 1914, she soon became noted for her excellent voice, her wit, striking beauty, and fine clothes. Despite her considerable talent, she was unpretentious. Beyond this scant information, little is known of the young girl who died tragically of influenza in 1918.

Taken as a whole, "Memorial to D. C." is not Millay at her best. Of the five separate poems in "Memorial," the "Epitaph" and "Dirge" lack Millay's usual subtle complexity. "Dirge" especially is too explicit:

> Boys and girls that held her dear,
> Do your weeping now;
> All you loved of her lies here.

There are some fine moments, however, in "Elegy" and "Chorus." The two controlling themes of "Memorial" are *philos* between women and a pantheistic type of rebirth. (*Philos* differs from *agape* in that *philos* is a deep friendship characterized by mutual respect and interest, whereas *agape* is a more divine love.) Millay views the death of Dorothy Coleman on several different levels—from supposed indifference to expressed grief over the loss of physical beauty and spiritual love to *philos*, in which the physical and spiritual merge.

In the "Chorus" of "Memorial to D. C.," Millay seems to feel more sorrow for the gowns and shoes than for the young woman herself. Again Millay is influenced by Sappho, who writes, "A broidered strap of fair Lydian work covered her feet," concerning the death of her young friend. Millay writes,

> Sweep her narrow shoes
> From the closet floor.

In "Dirge" Millay extends this objectification of grief into a mask of supposed indifference:

> Sing whatever songs are sung,
> Wind whatever wreath...."

In "Prayer to Persephone," Millay continues to view her friend objectively as she notes qualities—pride, arrogance, and flippancy—that would have been obvious to the casual observer.

Millay becomes more emotional as she equates Dorothy Coleman's death with the loss of physical beauty. In "Epitaph" she employs the image of a rose, an emblem of beauty and love:

> Heap not on this mound
>   Roses that she loved so well;
> Why bewilder her with roses,
>   That she cannot see or smell?

Then Millay grieves over the loss of Dorothy's physical beauty:

> Let them bury your big eyes
> In the secret earth securely,
> Your thin fingers, and your fair,
> Soft indefinite-coloured hair....
> Your young flesh that sat so neatly
> On your little bones....

(Millay later used equally sensual language to bemoan the eventual death of Arthur Davison Ficke in "And you as well must die, beloved dust.")

In "Prayer to Persephone," physical and spiritual love begin to merge:

> Be, to her, Persephone,
> All the things I might not be;
> Take her head upon your knee.
> She that was so proud and wild,
> Flippant, arrogant and free,
> She that had no need of me,
> Is a little lonely child
> Lost in Hell,–Persephone,
> Take her head upon your knee;
> Say to her, "My dear, my dear,
> It is not so dreadful here."

Millay implores Persephone to assume a maternal, protective role, to comfort Dorothy, "A little lonely child / Lost in Hell...." (Hell, of course, is another term for death.) Persephone is urged to "Take her head upon your knee," a protective gesture. When Millay refers to the young girl as "She that had no need of me," she may be referring to some lack of communication on the part of either woman. Yet the warmth of the relationship is suggested by the "little notes" Millay wrote her friend.

The final lines of "Elegy" serve as an effective conclusion to "Memorial," in which Millay merges physical and spiritual love for Dorothy, praising both the woman and her talent:

> All your lovely words are spoken.
> Once the ivory box is broken,
> Beats the golden bird no more.

(The "ivory box" refers to the body; the "golden bird" to Miss Coleman's voice.)

"Prayer to Persephone" is strongly suggestive of rebirth. Persephone, of course, was the daughter of Demeter, the goddess of corn, wheat, grain, and other vegetation. When Persephone, the goddess of spring, was carried away by the god of the underworld, Demeter caused a great famine to fall upon the earth. After a year of mankind's suffering, Zeus bade his brother Hermes descend into Hell to rescue Persephone. Before the god of the underworld released Persephone, he made her eat a pomegranate seed, which signified Persephone's eventual return to Hell. Upon Persephone's ascent, Demeter again made the fields rich with abundant crops, but she was sad when she learned that her daughter had to return to the underworld for four months of each year. Although Demeter suffered each time her daughter returned to Hell, the story contains a note of joy in that each spring flowers and wheat would come to life as Persephone rose from the underworld.

Thus, when Persephone comforts Dorothy Coleman, she may be attuning her to a temporary, rather than a permanent, death. In "Epitaph," Millay equates the young woman with roses, perhaps foreshadowing the line in "Dirge Without Music," "They are gone to feed the roses." In "Elegy," moreover, a continuum of life is strongly suggested: "All of these in some way, surely, / From the secret earth shall rise..." and "On and on eternally / Shall your altered fluid run...." Here rebirth is certainly not Christian rebirth but is perhaps a type of reincarnation related to pantheism.

In "Memorial to D. C.," Millay expressed her sapphic love and friendship for Dorothy Coleman, just as she explored her deeper love for Charlotte Babcock in *The Lamp and the Bell*. Millay's "sense of glad awakening" included not only her idea of Christian rebirth, so strong in "Renascence" and "God's World," but also the ability to love women unselfishly and completely in the finest classical sense. Even before her Vas-

sar days had ended, she was moving toward a more pantheistic concept of God and death.

As a child, Millay believed that death was followed by
Christian rebirth. But at Vassar, she was more drawn to pantheism than to orthodox Christianity. Millay's coterie, especially Charlotte Babcock and Dorothy Coleman, gave her a
glimpse of the power of love. Not until her days in the Village did she find her Phaon. But her Vassar *hetaerae* had
flashed across her body and soul—brilliant and fleeting as a
meteor—or as Millay expressed it more quietly in "Passer
Mortuus Est":

> Death devours all lovely things:
>> Lesbia with her sparrow
> Shares the darkness,—presently
>> Every bed is narrow....
>
> After all, my erstwhile dear,
>> My no longer cherished,
> Need we say it was not love,
>> Just because it perished?

2

WE WERE VERY TIRED,
WE WERE VERY MERRY:

An Overview
of the Village

After leaving the Waverly Theatre, winding down Cornelia
Street and passing the Cherry Lane Theatre, you stumble on
a half-lighted, unmarked courtyard. Walking through the
large black door, you are transported back to the 1920's,
when Chumley's Bar was a speakeasy and a mecca for writers,
painters, and actors who sat quietly and played chess.[1] Then,
as now, the walls of the dimly lighted, large room are neatly
lined with playbills casually imprinted with such names as
Norma Millay, Charles Ellis, and Eugene O'Neill, and dust
jackets bearing the names of e. e. cummings and Sherwood
Anderson. Both Norma and Edna Millay frequented Chumley's because Lee Chumley "served a good dollar dinner...."[2]
The bartender at Chumley's, Greg Garcia, said that Edna St.
Vincent Millay, after drinking too much gin or beer, was frequently escorted home late at night by one of her male
friends.[3]

Greenwich Village is a mass of "little twisted streets that
crossed and recrossed each other and never seemed to get
anywhere...."[4] In its center is Washington Square, a stretch
of green, bordered by a number of park benches, where one
can sit and read, talk, or do nothing at all. In the background

of Washington Square looms New York University. Before
Washington Square became a park in 1827, it had been "in
successive decades Potter's Field, parade grounds, place of
executions...."[5] During Millay's time, little delicatessens and
coffee shops helped to create an old European atmosphere in
the Village.

During the Pre-Twenties (1910-20)[6] the Villagers were
bound together by a repudiation of their basically middle-
class backgrounds. Nearly all the Villagers were college educated. Some—such as Edna St. Vincent Millay, Theodore
Dreiser, John Sloan, and Robert Henri—were serious in their
artistic pursuits,[7] but many merely were acting out the roles
of artists while being subsidized by a monthly check from
home. Some Villagers chose to create their masterpieces in
isolation, but many chose to become members of the Liberal
Club, the *Masses'* staff, or one of the little theater groups.

The Liberal Club was the social center of the Village. (Millay reveals her special interest in Macdougal Street, where
both the Liberal Club and the Provincetown Playhouse were
located, in "Macdougal Street.") Members of the club
included Floyd Dell, John Reed, Eugene O'Neill, Susan Glas-
pel, and Edna St. Vincent Millay, who wrote and produced
their plays for the club. Polly Holliday and Hippolyte Havel
gave a family atmosphere to the group by feeding them,
whether or not they could pay. Sometimes the Liberals had
an eccentric enjoyment of life; for example, shortly after
Floyd Dell arrived in New York, he met a dancer who kept a
pet alligator in her bathtub.[8] Gradually the Liberal Club dis-
solved into such little theater groups as the Provincetown
Players, under the leadership of George Cram (Jig) Cook, the
Washington Square Players, and the Cherry Lane Players.

At the center of the intellectual life of the Village was the
Masses, a magazine that advocated peace, socialism, and revolution. In 1913 Max Eastman left his position as professor of
philosophy at Columbia University to become editor of the

journal. Others associated with the magazine were John Reed, Art Young, John Sloan, and Floyd Dell, the managing editor. In the spirit of reform, the *Masses* published a story, illustrated by John Sloan, about a girl being beaten by the matron of a reformatory. When the magazine began a birth control campaign, they aroused the ire of Anthony Comstock, a leading Roman Catholic, who asked the police department to stop their propaganda. In October 1917, the editors of the *Masses* were indicted for violation of the Sedition Act, an offense that carried a sentence of twenty years, because they protested America's participation in World War I and contended that the Allies would not repay their loans.

For entertainment, the Villagers frequented speakeasies such as Chumley's, where local Italians sold liquor illegally. Other places of amusement included the cabarets and tearooms, but these were largely supported by tourists.[9] The Villagers visited the theater and listened to philharmonic concerts and political speeches on the radio, but they considered movies a cheap form of art, and they distained playing cards. They also enjoyed spontaneous all-night parties, where everyone simply slept where he happened to be. And always there were endless discussions about art, politics, and ethics. Floyd Dell explained, "I preferred to get drunk on ideas, on talk, on argument."[10] But the Villagers were not always so cerebral. One night Floyd Dell, Theodore Dreiser, and several girls stayed at Polly Holliday's until 1:00 a.m. playing a rowdy game of "Up Jenkins," no doubt capitalizing on its gambling potential, which sent Polly to bed with a headache and attracted three policemen from blocks away.

From 1910 to 1920 (Millay's era), the Village was the medium for artistic ferment. On February 17, 1913, the famous Armory Show opened in New York. Although the show was predominantly European, John Quinn asserted in his opening speech that American art was on the verge of drastic change: "The members of this Association have shown that American artists...do not dread and have no need to dread the ideas or culture of Europe."[11] Included in this avant-garde collection were paintings and sculpture of the Fauvanists, such as Matisse; the cubists, such as Picasso and Braque; and the futurists, such as Marcel Duchamps, his *Nude Descending a Staircase* being definitely representative of the futurists.

Public reaction to this show was puzzled and sometimes hostile. Former President Theodore Roosevelt remarked that *Nude Descending a Staircase* reminded him of a Navajo blanket. The American Art News sponsored a contest to find the nude in Duchamp's painting. But Duchamps was not the only artist to suffer the barbs of the philistines. When the exhibit was moved to Chicago, students at the Chicago Art Institute hanged Matisse in effigy and burned imitations of his paintings.

On March 8, 1913, Edna St. Vincent Millay visited the Armory Show. (Millay was attending Barnard College for one semester to prepare for her entrance to Vassar in September 1913.) Singularly unimpressed by the cubists, she thought their work looked "like a pile of shingles." She wrote her family, "I'll get some postals of the pictures...especially the one called 'Nude descending the stairs,' and if you can find the figure, outline it in ink and send it back to me." Floyd Dell told Norman Brittin in an interview that Millay was offended by "eccentricities in art and poetry" and by "willful defiance of tradition."

One of the most representative movements of this decade was Dadaism, a movement founded in Zurich in 1916 that was opposed to art, war, materialism, and rationalism. "Dada" is derived from a French nonsense syllable meaning "hobbyhorse," suggestive of meaningless back-and-forth motion and perhaps of nihilism. By 1917 Duchamps had abandoned futurism to become a Dadaist. His resignation from the Society of American Arts, of which he was vice-president, stemmed from their refusal of his sculpture *Fountain,* which he had made from a urinal. *L. H. O. O. Q.,* Duchamps' painting of Mona Lisa with a moustache, exemplifies the Dadaists' antiart trend, which often shocked the "cultured" art connoisseur. Millay echoes Dadaism, particularly its nihilistic tone, in "April / Comes like an idiot, babbling and strewing flowers."

John Sloan and Peter Blume were two Village artists who were influenced by European avant-garde trends during the Pre-Twenties. Sloan was a member of the Ash Can School, a movement more concerned with social than aesthetic revolt. Interested in depicting humble subjects, they burlesqued Whistler and extolled Whitman for his "democracy." Sloan's *Sunday, Women Drying Their Hair,* exhibited in the Armory Show, depicts three poorly dressed women drying their hair as they sit atop a dirty building with clothes hanging in the background. An avowed socialist, Sloan painted other scenes of lower-class life in *Hairdresser's Window, The Cot,* and *The Wake of the Ferry.* Due to a dispute with Floyd Dell, Sloan resigned as art editor of the *Masses* in 1916.

Although Millay did not know Sloan, she found beauty in the humble subjects that Sloan depicted in his paintings. During her 1913 stay in New York, she wrote her family on February 6:

> From my window in the daytime I can see *everything*...buildings everywhere...washing drying on the roofs and on lines strung between the houses....Children on roller skates playing tag on the sidewalks...and *noise*, yes, in New York you can *see* the noise.[12]

In her poem, "Macdougal Street," she celebrated the essential humanity of the local Italians amid the squalor of their environment.

Sharing Chumley's with Millay was Peter Blume, a lifelong friend of Malcolm Cowley. As a young artist, Blume was influenced by precisionism, an offshoot of cubism. Later Blume became one of the most important Magic Realists, art-

ists who found the reality of poverty, joblessness, and the
threat of war so oppressive that they escaped into the world
of the imagination. Blume's masterpiece, *South of Scranton*
(1931), depicts the mind's imagination in precise, photo-
graphic detail.[13]

Although Millay expressed deep annoyance with the cubists, she was affected by other avant-garde trends in painting
and sculpture in the Village. As she lost her orthodox Christian belief in God, nihilistic notes of Dadaism crept into her
poetry. Especially in "Macdougal Street" and "Recuerdo,"
Millay revealed the love for the common man that John
Sloan also exhibited in his works.

As early as the 1890's, the American novel was shifting
from the optimistic realism of the early and middle works of
Mark Twain to the naturalism of Stephen Crane, Frank Norris, and Theodore Dreiser. In 1893 Stephen Crane published
Maggie: A Girl of the Streets, America's first significant natu-
ralistic novel. Through his youthful admiration of Norris'
work and his friendship with Dreiser in Greenwich Village,
Floyd Dell was exposed to naturalism. Dell probably
explained his concepts of naturalism and atheism to Millay in
1918-19, but she retained her deep love of mankind—her new
concept of Christianity—a sharp contrast to the naturalist's
assumption that man is often doomed by nature.

Just as the Armory Show in 1913 signaled new trends in
painting and sculpture, 1912 had marked the beginning of a
metamorphosis in poetry with Harriet Monroe's *Poetry: A
Magazine of Verse* and Ferdinand Earle's *The Lyric Year*, a
contest to discover the best one hundred new poems. Monroe
and Earle were determined to reeducate the American public,
which was still transfixed by the sentimental poetry of Long-
fellow, Whittier, and Holmes. When Earle read Millay's
"Renascence," he wrote her immediately that she had won
the first prize of $500. His judgment, unfortunately, was pre-
mature; the other judges were not as impressed, and Millay

finally won fourth prize, which carried no monetary reward.

Harriet Monroe and the other editors of *Poetry* had three prohibitions: no poetic diction, no classical references, and no sonnets. As international editor, Ezra Pound introduced the imagists to *Poetry*. Amy Lowell became the American leader of the imagists, poets who encouraged free verse, precise imagery, and unlimited choice of subjects. The imagists also believed that poetry should be "hard and clear, never blurred and indefinite" and that "concentration is the very essence of poetry." One of Miss Lowell's best-known works is "Bath," a prose poem, which appeared in the anthology *Some Imagist Poets* in 1916:

> The sunshine pours in at the bathroom window and bores
> through the water in the bath-tub in lathes and planes
> of greenish white. It cleaves the water into flaws like
> a jewel, and cracks it to bright light.

Violent controversies arose between the experimentalists and the traditionalists. Leading the experimentalists were Amy Lowell, Ezra Pound, and T. S. Eliot. Active in resistance to the experimentalists were Arthur Davison Ficke and Witter Bynner. Ficke believed that free verse was a limited form, that the poet profited from having to work within a prescribed form, and that imagism was effective only when used in presenting detached details. Speaking to the Fortnightly Club, Chicago's oldest club for women, Bynner "worked off a long-cherished grudge against the imagists, hurling more adjectives at their devoted heads than one may find in all their poems."[14]

In 1916 Ficke and Bynner wrote the entire text of the *Spectra,* a volume of poems parodying free verse, in ten days with the aid of as many quarts of Scotch. Ficke decided to assume the identity of Anne Knish (a knish is a Jewish pastry), and Bynner became Emanuel Morgan (*morgen* is the German word for "morning," and the vague idea conveyed was "morning song"). Strikingly beautiful and mysterious,

Anne Knish loathed domesticity and her husband, whereas
Morgan was more stable—a middle-aged man with a square-
cut beard. Concealing the real identities of Knish and Morgan
for nearly two years, Ficke and Bynner (as themselves) perpe-
trated the hoax on every occasion; at least once, Bynner
boldly announced that the Spectrists were to poetry what
cubism was to painting. The hoax was so successful that the
Spectrists received plaudits from Harriet Monroe, William
Carlos Williams, Edgar Lee Masters, Alfred Kreymborg, and
Amy Lowell. Inadvertently, the Spectrists composed some
fine poetry, but a typical example of their work is Emanuel
Morgan's "Opus 104":

> How terrible to entertain a lunatic!
> To keep his earnestness from coming close!
> A Madagascar land-crab once
> Lifted blue claws at me
> And rattled long black eyes
> That would have got me
> Had I not been gay.

In *Exiles Return,* Malcolm Cowley commented that the
Villagers' rejection of conventional standards led to a "private war between Greenwich Village and the Saturday Evening Post...." Finding bourgeois morality and values irrele-
vant, the Villagers formulated their own codes of sexual and
social standards. Some of their concepts of women relate to
the Women's Liberation Movement of the 1970's: married
women should have independent interests and be self-sup-
porting; husbands should share in household tasks; children
are not necessary to a successful marriage; divorce should be
easier to obtain; and, unmarried couples should be allowed to
live together. The Villagers also foreshadowed the New
Morality of our era: they did not expect either a man or
woman to enter marriage as a virgin; some repudiated family
realtionships altogether. Dell and the girl he lived with for
several years shared these beliefs. In *Love in Greenwich Vil-*

lage, Dell says, "We held the same views of literature and art, we agreed in hating capitalism and war. And, incidentally, of course, we agreed in disbelieving in marriage. We considered it a stupid relic of the barbaric past...."

In his search for self-awareness, the Villager was intensely interested in psychoanalysis (particularly Freudianism), free association, emphasis upon deep seated emotions, recognition of unconquerable emotions, and sexual impulses in women as well as in men. He believed in a Wordsworthian salvation by the child (childlike innocence), paganism, living for the moment, and Puritanism as the great enemy. The Villager was generally not interested in acquiring money for its own sake, finding art a more meaningful approach to life than capitalism. Homosexuality and premarital sex were accepted Village norms. Other nonartistic inhabitants of the Village, especially uneducated Catholic Italians, regarded the Villagers as "a menace to the decency of their neighborhood and to the morals of their children."

In the Pre-Twenties, Millay became a living symbol of the freedom and hedonism of the Village. Cowley wrote that many men in the Village fell in love with Edna Millay, but he and Kenneth Burke fell in love with Norma.[15] Cowley suggested that Eugene O'Neill did not fall under the Millay spell, probably because of professional jealousy on both their parts. Still Burke and Cowley admired Edna Millay from afar, and in 1917 Burke wrote a series of limericks based on each of Millay's four names:

> I've told you the story today
> Of Edna St. Vincent Millay,
> While omitting the parts
> That would shatter men's hearts,
> Not befitting a bachelor to say.

> There was a young woman named Edna,
> Who had reddish hair on her headna....

> There was a young woman named Saint,
> Who was named for something she ain't....[16]

Edmund Wilson once told Edna Millay that her ex-admirers should form an alumni association. Even in the 1970's, the Millay Legend of the poet's beauty, genius, and hedonism (if indeed it is a legend) is strongly merged with the Millay Reality. Norma Millay Ellis is sometimes awakened by late-night calls from one of her young friends. He is an attractive, intelligent young bachelor in the East. Once he said to Mrs. Ellis, "Norma, it is not to you I speak...."[17] This young man's almost supernatural statement suggests both the spiritual bond young people still share with Edna Millay and the continuing vitality of her free spirit, which so attracted her suitors in the village.

As a member of the Liberal Club and as a friend of Floyd Dell and John Reed, both on the staff of the *Masses,* Millay was exposed to the socialism that pervaded the Village. But Millay did not develop a strong sense of social consciousness, such as her concern with war and her anguish over the Sacco-Vanzetti trial, until much later. In the Village, Millay was not actively involved in political activities, although Floyd Dell "earnestly discoursed upon Pacificism, Revolution, Soviet Russia, and Psychoanalysis to her." She regarded Freudian ideas as "a Teutonic attempt to lock women up in the home and restrict them to cooking and baby-tending."

With the Provincetown Players, Millay found an outlet for both acting and playwriting. Millay performed in Alfred Kreymborg's *Manikin and Minikin,* Wallace Stevens' *Three Travelers Watch a Sunrise,* Floyd Dell's *The Angel Intrudes* and *Sweet-and-Twenty,* and many other plays. The three Millay sisters, Edna, Norma, and Kathleen, sang the offstage chorus for Eugene O'Neill's *Moon of the Caribbees*, and they sometimes broke into a folk song about cocaine.[18] In 1919 Millay helped direct her own *Aria da Capo*, in which Norma played Columbine and Charles Ellis, later to become Norma's husband, played one of the shepherds.

As far as Millay's poetry was concerned, the imagists and T. S. Eliot had little, if any, effect on Millay's work. Millay and Arthur Davison Ficke, a leader of the traditionalists, exchanged and admired each other's poetry. As a poet, John Peale Bishop felt Millay was "at her best when most conventional." The strict form of the sonnet, which was quite unpopular in the early 1920's, provided an exacting form that forced Millay to find the precise word, emotion, and tone for her moving love sonnets.

Although the form of Millay's poems did not correspond with avant-garde trends, her subject matter was related to contemporary thought. As previously mentioned, "Spring" contains a note of Dadaism. Millay became an avowed feminist during 1917-18. Many were horrified and some were delighted by such lines as,

> After all's said and after all's done,
> What should I be but a harlot and a nun?

Millay had no desire to become "domestic as a plate" and was pleased that "My true love is false!"

Millay was not overwhelmed by the new philosophy she found in the Village. Always maintaining her individual integrity, she selected values that she considered relevant and discarded others. Like many other Villagers, she attended plays, concerts, operas, and speakeasies, with the evening sometimes culminating in parties that lasted until dawn. She also agreed with the Villagers' concepts of the liberated woman and freer attitudes toward sex. But Millay did not share the Villagers' contempt for money. In a letter to Harriet Monroe, Millay added a postscript: "I am *awfully* broke. Would you mind paying me a lot?" When she did not make enough money from her serious poetry and drama, she wrote popular articles for *Ainslee's* and *Vanity Fair* under the pseudonym Nancy Boyd.[19] (Millay wrote over twenty Nancy Boyd pieces—nine stories, the rest poetry—which comprise roughly one-fourth of her total work.) Gladys Brown Ficke said Millay was very secure about her ability to make money.

Greenwich Village served as the catalyst for two important transformations in the life and works of Edna St. Vincent Millay: she developed a new concept of Christianity, and she sought to liberate women from their traditional roles. Leaving the relatively protective, conservative environments of Camden and Poughkeepsie, Millay encountered a diverse group of people in New York. Being exposed to some of the most avant-garde thought of the day, Millay readily discarded many of the traditional, repressive aspects of Christianity, began to respect humble people, and developed an almost Whitmanesque love of mankind. Not only was she exposed to her intellectual friends such as Arthur Davison Ficke, Witter Bynner, Eugene O'Neill, and Wallace Stevens and her educated, politically active friends such as Edmund Wilson, Floyd Dell, and John Reed, she also observed the common man, such as the local Italian, for whom she developed a particular love.

Threads of Millay's new Christiantiy wind throughout *A Few Figs from Thistles* and *Second April*. In "Macdougal Street," Millay paints a sympathetic picture of the local Italians. "Recuerdo" contains a moving vignette of an old shawl-covered woman. The "Poet and His Book," "Alms," and "The Little Hill" all reveal Millay's new Christianity.

In "Macdougal Street," the slight story of the friendship between two Italians—a little girl and an older man—suggests a beauty and love that rises out of the squalor:

> As I went walking up and down to take the evening air,
>   (Sweet to meet upon the street, why must I be so shy?)
> I saw him lay his hand upon her torn black hair;
>   ("Little dirty Latin child, let the lady by!")

The narrator is caught in the dirty, yet vital, atmosphere of the street as she notices the fat women, lazy cats, babies, and carts:

> The fruit-carts and clam-carts were ribald as a fair,
>   (Pink nets and wet shells trodden under heel).

The little girl haggles with the fruitmen and throws a curse at the older man; he in turn tousles her hair. Their love, the vitality of the street, her love of mankind so move the narrator that she exclaims, "(I wish I were a ragged child with earrings in my ears!)."

In "Recuerdo," Millay describes a midnight ferry ride to Staten Island with one of her Village suitors. Her *joie de vivre* and love of mankind is captured in the first stanza:

> We were very tired, we were very merry—
> We had gone back and forth all night on the ferry.
> It was bare and bright, and smelled like a stable—
> But we looked into a fire, we leaned across a table,
> We lay on a hill-top underneath the moon;
> And the whistles kept blowing, and the dawn came soon.

In the last stanza, she creates a vignette of an old woman who sells newspapers on the street. Despite their enjoyment of their own escapade, the narrator and her friend pause to buy a newspaper, which they do not read, from the old woman, give her all their fresh fruit, and all their money but their subway fares. As they leave, the tattered woman weeps in gratitude.[20]

In "The Poet and His Book," Millay urges her readers, "Read me, margin me with scrawling, / Do not let me die!" Celebrating young lovers, she implores them to give her works new life through their affection and spontaneity:

> Boys and girls that lie
>   Whispering in the hedges,
> Do not let me die,
>   Mix me with your pledges;
> Boys and girls that slowly walk
>   In the woods, and weep, and quarrel,
>   Staring past the pink wild laurel,
> Mix me with your talk....

She shows her love for men of humble professions—farmers,

shepherds, sailors, and hunters—as well as for scholars, and she implores housewives to "Mix me with your grief!" By suggesting that she and her works can continue to exist only through this microcosm of people, she exhibits a Whitman-esque respect and love for all mankind.

Millay's new concept of Christianity is more explicit in "Alms":

> I loved the beggar that I fed,
> I cared for what he had to say....

"The Little Hill" recalls the suffering and anguish of Christ's crucifixion. Despite the universal scope of this event, Millay chooses to concentrate on the human aspect of grief: "Remember Mary's tears." Millay's new Christianity is best summed up by the poet in a letter to her mother in 1917: "I picked up a spilled bundle for a woman the other day—her arms were so full she could hardly bend—& carried it for her a couple of blocks—& she blessed me as if I were an angel...."

Millay is at her best in her love poems, which she began writing in the Village. Her series of *Twenty Sonnets,* published in *Reedy's Mirror* during April and May of 1920, were broken up and placed in *A Few Figs from Thistles, Second April,* and even *The Harp-Weaver* (1923). Included in these sonnets were "Into the golden vessel of great song," "Not with libations," "Oh think not I am faithful to a vow," "And you as well must die, beloved dust," "Cherish you then the hope I shall forget," "Only until this cigarette is ended," "I do but ask that you be always fair," and "Euclid alone has looked on beauty bare."

In *I Thought of Daisy,* Edmund Wilson describes Millay's transformation in the Village as a "revolt of the individ-ual...." Especially in *A Few Figs from Thistles,* Millay sought to free women from their traditional submissive role. She was not merely being flippant when she wrote,

> "I've been a wicked girl," said I;
> "But if I can't be sorry, why,
> I might as well be glad!"

Millay urged women to be individuals in their own right. She liberated women writers from restrictions on what they could write about love and faithfulness and domesticity. Malcolm Cowley felt that Millay revolted against "the conventions that kept women from living honestly or recklessly." Harriet Monroe considers Millay's poetry "the most feminine sonnets ever written to prove the essential separateness of a woman's soul."

What most readers found shocking in Millay's Village poetry was the concept of sexual freedom for women. Millay is explicit and somewhat callous in "I shall forget you presently, my dear":

> But so it is, and nature has contrived
> To struggle on without a break thus far,—
> Whether or not we find what we are seeking
> Is idle, biologically speaking.

In "Only until this cigarette is ended," Millay uses the cigarette as a rather obvious symbol of passion; when the passion (cigarette) is spent, it falls in ashes:

> Only until this cigarette is ended,
> A little moment at the end of all,
> While on the floor the quiet ashes fall,
> And in the firelight to a lance extended,
> Bizarrely with the jazzing music blended,
> The broken shadow dances on the wall,
> I will permit my memory to recall
> The vision of you, by all my dreams attended.

Her lover in this sonnet has no clear identity, just as the lads in "What lips my lips have kissed" are "unremembered":

> Yours is a face of which I can forget
> The colour and the features, every one,
> The words not ever, and the smiles not yet....

In still another sonnet, Millay mocks unrealistic lovers' vows, perhaps even marriage vows:

> So wanton, light and false, my love, are you,
> I am most faithless when I most am true.

An important aspect of women's new sexual freedom was complete honesty—no longer were feminine wiles acceptable. In "I shall forget you presently," Millay says,

> If you entreat me with your loveliest lie
> I will protest you with my favorite vow....

She then says that oaths are brittle. In another sonnet, Millay requests,

> I do but ask that you be always fair,
> That I forever may continue kind....

In a much later poem (from *Fatal Interview*), the idea of honesty is more explicit:

> If I had loved you less or played you slyly
> I might have held you for a summer more....

In accordance with Village norms, Millay felt that women should have independent interests and should not consider themselves creatures of domesticity. Always an enemy of housework, Millay rejects the image of the submissive housewife in "Grown-Up":

> Was it for this I uttered prayers,
> And sobbed and cursed and kicked the stairs,
> That now, domestic as a plate,
> I should retire at half-past eight?

In "Portrait by a Neighbor," Millay again discredits domesticity, finding instead an Elizabethan beauty in disorder:

> Her lawn looks like a meadow,
>   And if she mows the place
> She leaves the clover standing
>   And the Queen Anne's lace!

In the search for the liberation of women, Millay insists on intellectual equality:

> Oh, oh, you will be sorry for that word!
> Give back my book and take my kiss instead.
> Was it my enemy or my friend I heard,
> "What a big book for such a little head!"

(This sonnet was first published in April 1922 in *Vanity Fair* and later appeared in *The Harp-Weaver*.) In many ways, Millay was the first American feminist. Not content with mere outward tokens of women's freedom, she sought real intellectual and emotional liberation of women. In her poetry, especially the sonnets, Bishop felt Millay achieves "a minute accuracy in the statement of emotion." The Millay Legend approaches the Millay Reality when the following statement by Harold Cook is considered: "She [Millay] approaches poetry from its emotional side, treating her subject, even when it is intellectual, emotionally....She seldom writes on a subject that has not moved *her* deeply...."

In the Village, Millay did not choose to become active in politics, to follow the precepts of the imagists, or to view money with contempt. But notes of Dadaism crept into her poetry, and she was moved by the humble subjects of the Ash Can School. The Village served as a catalyst for two important transformations in her life. Discarding the stern doctrines of Christianity, as seen in "Interim" and "The Suicide," Millay developed a new concept of religion—an all embracing love of mankind. She was consumed also by the search for individual freedom—sexual freedom, especially for women, and the right of women to become real individuals.

New York offered Millay a new type of freedom. Away from Camden and Poughkeepsie, Millay observed, "There is a beautiful anonymity about life in New York." In "Recuerdo," Millay revels in the freedom of riding the ferry until the "sun rose dripping, a bucketful of gold," but she is not ashamed to show her love for a fellow human being:

> We were very tired, we were very merry—
> We had gone back and forth all night on the ferry.
> We hailed, "Good morrow, mother!" to a shawl-covered head,
> And bought a morning paper, which neither of us read;
> And she wept, "God bless you!" for the apples and pears,
> And we gave her all our money but our subway fares.

Barrow Street entrance to courtyard of Chumley's Bar.

Courtyard and entrance to Chumley's Bar.

Interior of Chumley's Bar.

Entrance to Provincetown Playhouse.

Interior of Provincetown Playhouse.

Entrance to Cherry Lane Theatre.

Courtyard behind Millay's house at 75½ Bedford Street.

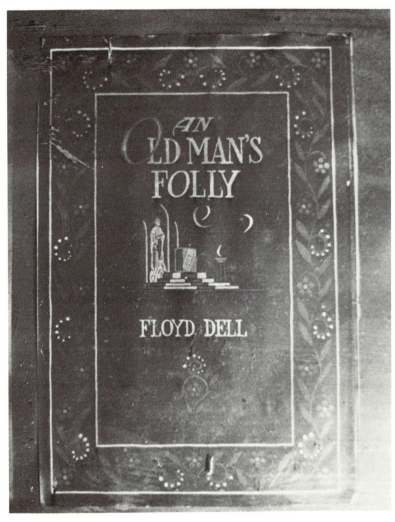

Dust jackets on walls of Chumley's Bar.

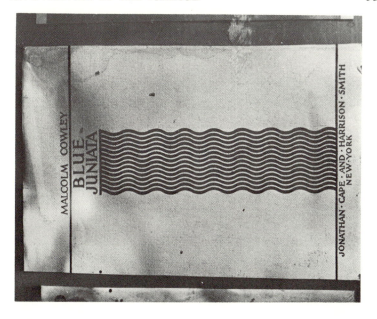

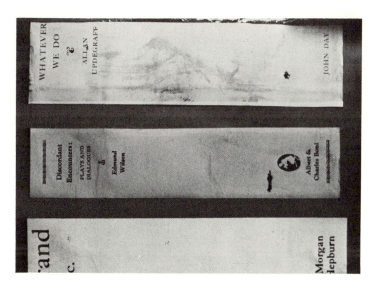

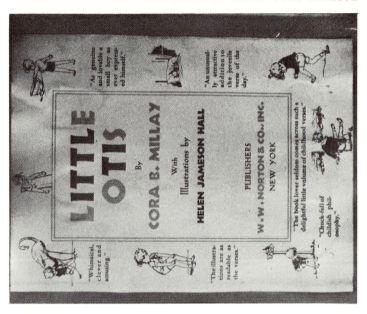

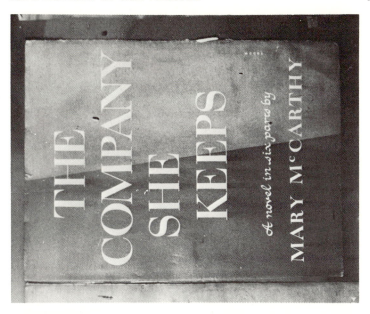

3

THIS DOOR YOU
MIGHT NOT OPEN:

Floyd Dell

One summer day Edna Millay dashed out of the Province-town Playhouse and swerved around the corner of Macdougal Street, laughing, her long auburn hair swinging about her face. Stopping to catch his breath, then rushing, stumbling, laughing, Floyd Dell chased the small, agile poet through narrow streets. Tall and lanky, craggy-faced and serious, Dell raced onward past unkempt Italian immigrants, brushed against clam carts and vegetable carts, but could not catch Millay. Evading the serious advances of this divorced man five years her senior, Millay perhaps threw back her head and shouted, "To heel, Apollo." Later Phyllis Duganne recounted this frivolity of 1918 to Edmund Wilson, who felt that it might well have served as the germ for "Daphne," which Millay published in the fall of the same year.

Light and musical in tone, "Daphne" is Millay's complaint against meddlers. Having failed in his first marriage, Dell was undergoing psychoanalysis in hopes of finding the perfect wife and urged Millay to undergo treatment in order to overcome her lesbian tendencies. But Millay, freed from the restrictive atmosphere of Vassar, had no intention of surrendering her freedom to her first serious Village suitor.

Assuming that "Daphne" does reflect Millay's relationship with Dell, then Millay in the role of Daphne, the beautiful, independent huntress, compares Dell, somewhat to his detriment, to Apollo. Daphne, similar to chaste Diana, distressed her father, Peneus, because she refused the love and marriage proposals of many handsome young men who wooed her. But one day Apollo saw her, and her carefree life was ended as she began running in fear, because women who bore children of the gods risked exile or death. As Apollo began to gain on the fleeing maiden, she called out in terror to her father, a river god, for help. Suddenly she felt rooted to the ground; she had escaped her pursuer by turning into a pink-blossomed laurel tree. In the first two stanzas of "Daphne," Millay recounts her flight from Dell:

> Why do you follow me?—
> Any moment I can be
> Nothing but a laurel-tree.
>
> Any moment of the chase
> I can leave you in my place
> A pink bough for your embrace.

In the last stanza, however, reality diverges from myth, as Millay taunts Dell with little of the respect Daphne granted Apollo:

> Yet if over hill and hollow
> Still it is your will to follow,
> I am off;—to heel, Apollo!

Although Floyd Dell was too talkative and cloying to be the perfect man for Millay, he was nevertheless an important Village influence, especially as her first heterosexual lover. Serious, analytical, and questioning, Floyd Dell is often considered the representative man of his times. His political activism, socialism, ostensible atheism, and deep interest in the literature of Frank Norris and Theodore Dreiser, his drinking companion, marked Dell as one of the more rebellious and thoughtful Villagers. Also a champion of women's rights and a critic of marriage, Dell perhaps planted the seeds of feminism in Millay's psyche. Before he met Millay, Dell shared an apartment with a young woman, a life style that they both jealously guarded, as Dell recounts in *Love in Greenwich Village*:

> We were not going to lie to please them, much less get married for their convenience....After all, we despised such people, and what they thought did not matter to us.

In *Homecoming,* however, Dell seems to waver in his enthusiasm for a "free love" relationship. Although the hero and heroine of the autobiography decline to marry as a matter of principle, Dell musingly thinks, "A serious love affair...might shatter with its reality many intellectual theories with which it has been approached."

In "The Button," a whimsical short story in *Love in Greenwich Village,* Dell again voices his strong approval of women's rights. Barbara Locke, an aspiring writer, leaves her husband because he insists that she sew a button on his coat, a request which stirs her loathing for domesticity.

> When a girl married, she became—a wife. She ceased to be a person. And what was worse, by some terrible alchemy which marriage brought, she didn't care. She was happy in just being that man's wife. She gave up her name. She lived in and through him. She had no life of her own; she existed to love him, and comfort him and sew his buttons on. That was all a man wanted of a woman. Well, she wouldn't be a wife. That was settled. She was going to write.

Aware of Millay's serious devotion to poetry, Dell felt that Eugen Boissevain was "a divinely ordained husband...for a girl poet, who would certainly not remember to darn his socks...."[1]

As an adolescent, Dell seemed squeamish about sex, "a mysterious and rather sacred theme, to be discussed impersonally in scientific terms, or solemnly and beautifully in poetic paraphrase."[2] But Dell was bolder about sex in *Love in Greenwich Village* as he praised Fan, a Southern girl, who moved to the Village because her Episcopal priest had commented with alarm that the Villagers "kept house together with out being married, and...separated without asking anybody's permission!" By the time Dell met Millay, he found beauty and dignity in heterosexual love and yearned "to be set free to love deeply enough to get married and have children...."[3]

When Millay met Dell in 1917, the winter in Greenwich Village was cold and miserable. Malcolm Cowley wrote, "The houses were cold because of fuel rationing, the faces were glum because of the war, the drinking was somber at the Hell Hole, and always there was the fear of the police."[4] After the fiasco of graduation from Vassar in June 1917, Millay spent the summer in Camden, visited Connecticut in the fall, and arrived in New York in September. For several months she lived on East 52nd Street and tried to get a job as an actress but failed uptown. After reading for a part in Dell's play in December, Edna and her sister Norma moved to the Village in January 1918. Four years earlier, Floyd Dell had come to New York to try his hand as a newspaper reporter, playwright, and novelist and had become a member of both the Liberal Club and the Provincetown Players, led by Jig Cook. With Dell's encouragement, Millay joined both groups in 1917.

When Floyd Dell advertised for a girl to play the ingenue part of Annabelle in *The Angel Intrudes,* which Malcolm Cowley considered "a forgettable one-act comedy," Millay came to the greenroom over the stable on Macdougal Street to audition. Enchanted by this "slender little girl with red-gold-hair," Dell immediately hired her "At a salary of nothing at all...."[5] She left her name and address, and Dell wondered if "Edna Millay" were the famous poet and soon discovered that she was indeed the author of "Renascence."

When *The Angel Intrudes* opened on December 28, 1917,

the Provincetown Players were so impressed with Millay's
performance that they immediately voted her a full member
of the company.[6] Pleased with his protégé, Dell then asked
Millay to play Helen, the coy and intelligent heroine of his
one-act play *Sweet and Twenty*, a satire on marriage. After
reading the play, Millay dashed off the music for the song
"April-May," which she glided on stage singing on opening
night, January 25, 1918.

> When I was sixteen no more than a day,
> > April-May!
> I met a young man in the flush of the moon.
> > May-June!
> His step was light and his manner was gay,
> > April-May!
> And he came from afar, by the dust on his shoon.
> > May-June!

In *Sweet and Twenty,* George and Helen, the young
couple, meet as they are inspecting a house that each hopes
to buy, and they fall in love even before they know each
other's name. Dell apparently was an advocate of love at first
sight; Felix fell hopelessly and instantly for Joyce in *Moon-
Calf*, just as Dell was immediately enchanted by Millay's coy-
ness and beauty. But this initial bliss seems to wane when
Helen insists that George must learn to dance and George
asks Helen to learn about socialism and "municipal owner-
ship of street cars." This situation mirrors the eventual conflict between Millay and Dell, the more coldly cerebral and
less spontaneous lover. Dell frequently mentions that he
could not dance—although his psychoanalyst later freed him
to do so—and he lectured Millay on socialism and pacifism.
George and Helen finally agree that the only common taste
they share is being in love with each other.

In the midst of their discussion, the Agent, really an
escaped inmate of an insane asylum, rushes on stage, obviously more interested in philosophy than in realty. Reading

George Bernard Shaw has not only driven him to insanity, but also to the bigamy of fourteen marriages! The Agent curses marriage as "an iniquitous arrangement devised by the Devil himself for driving all the love out of the hearts of lovers" and considers marriage as outdated an institution as a picnic. Man seemingly picnics—and marries—because "there is an instinct in us which makes us go back to the ways of our savage ancestors...." The only rationale for marriage, the Agent concludes, is to appease "civilization," or society, but as an alternative to marriage, he advises,

> If you are wise, you will build yourselves a little nest secretly in the woods, away from civilization, and you will run away together to that nest whenever you are in the mood. A nest so small that it will hold only two beings and one thought—the thought of love. And then you will come back refreshed to civilization...and...forget each other, and do your own work in peace.

At times *Sweet and Twenty* seems didactic, unevenly constructed, and frothy, but the play is a valuable reflection of Floyd Dell's views on marriage. Since he wrote the play after meeting Millay, it may well describe certain aspects of their early relationship. By encouraging Millay to perform in *The Angel Intrudes* and *Sweet and Twenty*, Floyd Dell advanced her admittedly short-lived career as an actress, but more importantly he initiated her into the Village milieu and exposed her to his attitudes toward marriage.

Interspersed with spirited discussions of love, marriage, and women's total identity, Floyd Dell and Edna Millay also explored more purely intellectual topics, such as creativity, socialism, and pacifism. Early in their relationship, he told her he realized that "Renascence," which he greatly admired, was written at two different times and furthermore that he knew when she had written each section. Millay said, "I don't suppose...that anyone could tell where the two parts are joined together," but after a day's meditation he discovered the split in "Renascence," later remarking, "She was greatly astonished and a little in awe of my uncanny critical powers."[7]

Dell not only respected Millay the woman but also Millay the artist. He found *Aria da Capo* to be "profoundly beautiful," "Renascence" "beautiful and astonishing," and several times echoed Millay's work in his own poetry. In "Child of the lightning," Dell's lines "your hands to touch the sky / Reach up..." closely resemble a phase from "Renascence," "And reaching up my hand to try, / I screamed to feel it touch the sky." Twice in "Christopher Street," which he included in *Love in Greenwich Village*, Dell refers to candles: "With your candles lit..." and "I've the candlestick...." In her famous "First Fig," Millay uses the candle as a symbol of the beauty and transience of life in the Village:

> My candle burns at both ends;
>   It will not last the night;
> But ah, my foes, and oh, my friends—
>   It gives a lovely light!

Finally, Dell's line, "The World is wide..." is similar to the last stanza of "Renascence":

> The world stands out on either side
> No wider than the heart is wide;
> Above the world is stretched the sky,—
> No higher than the soul is high.

As a literary critic, Millay was generally more precise and thoughtful than Dell. Basically preferring more traditional poetry, they both could appreciate imagism and free verse, Dell especially admiring the poetry of Ezra Pound:

> Professors have never annotated you, Ezra Pound, and silly old bibliopiles have never collected you in first editions and fine bindings. Nobody admires you whose admiration should cause us to suspect you.[8]

Although Millay finally recommended e. e. cummings for a Guggenheim Fellowship, she was exasperated with the personality behind his poetry:

> For if ever I disliked a man without ever having laid eyes on him, it is this same e. e. cummings....My judgement is as follows: here is a big talent, in the hands of an arrogant, peevish, self-satisfied and self-indulgent writer. That is to say here is a big talent in pretty bad hands. Mr. Cummings may do anything he likes with the alphabet, the English grammar, and the multiplication table, provided only the result...be...interesting, and...comprehensible....

Grudgingly Millay admitted that in cummings' book "there is fine writing and powerful writing...," and she mentioned specific cummings' poems that she admired:

> Mr. Cummings in love, for instance, his arrogance for the moment subdued, his spirit troubled and humbled, can produce such beautiful poems as are to be found in parts IV and V of "Is 5."[9]

The literary essays of Millay and Dell reflect facets of their works and personalities. Dell's criticism of Pound is very general and ignores subtleties of poetry, just as Dell tended to be verbose and at times didactic. In her criticism of cummings, Millay comments precisely about tone, subject matter, and style, reflecting the highly polished and chiseled quality of her poetry, especially the sonnets. Finally, Dell's criticism reflects the romanticism and seriousness of his personality, while Millay seems sharply realistic and humorous.

A man of ideas, Floyd Dell embraced socialism, pacifism, human individualism, and perhaps atheism at an early age. As a child Dell was disturbed when his mother would not let him play with a little Negro boy: "I took seriously the story about my father having fought and suffered in the war to set free the slaves."[10] Millay's poignant vignettes of the unkempt Italians in "Macdougal Street," the tattered woman in "Recuerdo," farmers, scholars, and young lovers in "The Poet and His Book" all reflect the deep sense of human individualism that Millay shared with Dell. Influenced by the works of Frank Norris and George Bernard Shaw and the convictions of George Cram Cook, director of the Province-town Players, Dell gave vent to his socialist beliefs in the "radical" magazine, the *Masses*. In *Aria da Capo*, her antiwar play, Millay voiced her basic objection to socialism through Pierrot: "I am become a socialist. I love humanity; but / I hate people." Although she later became deeply concerned with America's role in World War II, Millay was basically indifferent to politics while in the Village; she exclaimed to Witter Bynner in 1920, "The people of this country are just electing a new Sacred Goat."[11] At sixteen Dell was introduced to atheism, which he felt was "a natural part of Socialism." But he did not remain committed, later musing in *Moon-Calf*, "You proved that Atheists were fools, and that Christians were fools, in just the same way." Millay remained unaffected by Dell's atheism, always retaining her deep love of mankind, her new Christianity.

Although Dell was a man of diverse intellectual pursuits, he also considered emotional stability and happiness important aspects of life. Encouraged by his success with psychoanalysis, he was sometimes overly insistent that his friends seek similar treatment. At times he was meddlesome, chatty, and indiscreet; for example, he divulged intimate details of his divorce to Arthur Davison Ficke.

As Dell came to know Millay more intimately, he became alarmed at her preoccupation with lesbianism:

> With some of her poems she was...to give dignity and sweetness to those passionate friendships between girls in adolescence....

Dell felt that Millay was trapped in "the enchanted garden of childhood," which excluded males. At twenty-five, Millay was "terrified at the bogeys which haunt the realm of grown up man-and-woman love...." Dell urged her to seek psychological therapy to overcome her lesbiaism,[12] but she refused, being "hostile to Freudian ideas" as "a Teutonic attempt to lock women up in the home and restrict them to cooking and baby-tending."[13]

As Millay's first male lover, Floyd Dell played an important role in shaping Millay's attitude toward the relationship of sex to love, an important concept in her love poetry. Millay seemed to prefer sexual experiences with men to those with women after her first encounter with Dell, but she nevertheless resented his intrusion into her innermost thoughts and being. But without Dell's intrusion, Millay might never have understood the necessity of physical love for a deep spiritual union. Some of the men she was later involved with remained purely physical objects to her. In "I being born a woman and distressed," she says of a past lover: "I find this frenzy insufficient reason / For conversation when we meet again." Yet with the men most important to her—Dell, Wilson, Ficke, and Boissevain—she was increasingly able to fuse sexual love with spiritual love.

Sharing Dell's hatred of war, Millay gave him moral support by attending the second *Masses'* trial in October 1918, which was similar to the first trial six months earlier. Dell and three other members of the *Masses'* staff, Max Eastman, John Reed, and Art Young, were tried for conspiracy to promote insubordination and mutiny in the military forces. Having written that war was immoral and that the allies would not repay their loans, Dell and his colleagues were subject to twenty years in prison and fines of $10,000 each; their sole defense rested in the right of freedom of the press. The entire jury had admitted to a prejudice against socialists and conscientious objectors but had been retained when they said that they could overcome their prejudices. As in the first trial, the court required each man to read aloud his supposedly treasonous works and to explain his particular views. After explaining his ideas on war, militarism, conscientious objectors, especially his Thoreavian statement, "There are some laws that the individual feels he cannot obey," Dell found the cross-examination "a primitive game of wits." Just as the first trial had been postponed because of a deadlock, the case was dismissed in the second trial with the jury deadlocked six to six.

Even before Millay moved to the Village in 1918, she had conceived the idea for *Aria da Capo*, an indictment of both war and "man's folly, his greed, his quarrels, his war-like games."[14] As Corydon and Thyrsis tend their sheep, they decide to break the tranquility by playing a game:

> I know a game worth two of that
> Let's gather rocks, and build a wall between us;
> And say that over there belongs to me,
> And over here to you!

After weaving a wall of colored crepe paper, their game becomes increasingly serious and ugly. After Corydon discovers that all the water is on Thyrsis' side, he begs him for a drink for his sheep, but Corydon replies, "Well, they're not my sheep." Then Corydon refuses to share his new-found jewels with Thyrsis, until he, with no thought for his sheep, is thirsty himself. The deadly game finally leads to the destruction of both shepherds; Thyrsis gives Corydon a bowl of poisoned water, and Corydon strangles Thyrsis with a jeweled necklace. One year after the *Masses'* trial, Millay directed the first performance of *Aria da Capo* at the Provincetown Playhouse. Although Floyd Dell did not influence the plot of the play, he perhaps encouraged Millay's pacifist tendencies as she completed the final draft.

Enchanted by this young woman caught between adolescence and adulthood, Dell became a serious suitor of Millay in the Village, at times finding her "a scared little girl from Maine," at other times "an austere immortal, a goddess." Dell convinced her that she should become involved in the struggle for equal rights for women, but that her deepest feelings should be reserved for men. From her college days, Millay had been a champion of Inez Milholland. Once Dell gave Millay a bronze button, which was awarded to women who had been arrested and imprisoned for their suffragette activities. "Tears came into her eyes. 'I would rather have the right to wear this than anything I can think of,' she said." Not only

did Floyd Dell provide Millay with male companionship himself, he also introduced her to two men who were to play
important roles in her life—Arthur Davison Ficke and Eugen
Boissevain. After *Second April*, which contains poems from
Millay's earliest Village days, she ceased to write poems with
lesbian themes. In *Wine from These Grapes* Millay included
"Sappho Crosses the Dark River into Hades," but this poem
concerns Sappho's relation to Phaon rather than to her
hetaerae, or young girls.

In *The Poet and Her Book*, Jean Gould comments that Millay wrote her sonnet "Bluebeard" to Floyd Dell as an indictment of his meddling, but "Bluebeard" was first published in
Forum more than a year before Millay first met Dell at the
audition for *The Angel Intrudes*. Yet the sonnet does reflect
Millay's basic resentment of an inquisitive person such as
Floyd Dell, a theme that recurs in her Nancy Boyd pieces.

"Bluebeard" is a bitter condemnation of invasion of privacy. Throughout the octave, the first part of the sonnet, the
narrator mocks the man who had forced his way into her
most private thoughts and emotions:

> This door you might not open, and you did;
> So enter now, and see for what slight thing
> You are betrayed....Here is no treasure hid,
> No cauldron, no clear crystal mirroring
> The sought-for Truth, no heads of women slain
> For greed like yours, no writhings of distress;
> But only what you see....Look yet again:
> An empty room, cobwebbed and comfortless.

She tells him that there is no treasure nor beheaded women
behind the door he has so rudely forced open, but rather "An
empty room, cobwebbed and comfortless." Twice she breaks
her subtle, jeering tone when she refers to his betrayal and
greed.

In the sestet of "Bluebeard," the narrator is more caustic
and resentful of the man's probing:

> Yet this alone out of my life I kept
> Unto myself, lest any know me quite;
> And you did so profane me when you crept
> Unto the threshold of this room tonight
> That I must never more behold your face.
> This now is yours. I seek another place.

"This alone" may refer to Millay's attitude toward women or merely to the thoughts that one must keep to oneself. Finally feeling profaned and violated by such a curious and demanding person, the narrator rejects him completely and leaves the tarnished dream for him to explore alone: "This now is yours. I seek another place."

Although Millay wrote "Bluebeard" before she met Dell, the sonnet still reveals her reaction to a persistent man with ideas very different from her own. Just when she had found her freedom in the Village, Millay had no desire to settle down to a typical married life with a man five years her senior. Her feelings of pain and resentment toward Dell are understandable; most major changes in behavior involve considerable emotional and intellectual expense. Dell delved too deeply into Millay's psyche, so she rejected him. But he significantly shaped the future of both Millay the woman and Millay the artist—by affording her a glimpse of heterosexual love, he freed her to write some of the most beautiful love sonnets in the English language.

"Child of the lightning," Dell's sonnet written to Millay, reveals that his love for her was much more serious than hers for him:

> Child of the lightning, alien to our dust,
> We seek you in the tempest—you are there,
> Drenched with the storm of beauty, gust on gust
> Of poignant sweetness only you can bear.
> Startled, you vanish in the darkness, fleeing
> The too-close human handclasp; you are fain
> Of the caresses native to your being—
> Strange joys that wound intolerably with pain.

> But all in vain your hands to touch the sky
> Reach up, in vain your bosom to the thunders
> Bared—there is only you and mayhap I
> And the old commonplace authentic wonders
> Of food and fire and bed. There's no use trying.
> So back you come, and yet—Why, you are crying!

In the octave, Dell celebrates Millay's immortal, goddess-like qualities by comparing her to the lightning, tempests, and storms. Then she assumes more human characteristics, being frightened, confused, running. The line "Strange joys that wound intolerably with pain" has clear heterosexual overtones. In the sestet, Millay's spiritual and physical qualities merge as her "hands to touch the sky / Reach up...." As the poem closes, Millay comes out of the storm of beauty and darkness into the warmth of humanity—"food and fire and bed." As a final proof of her transition from immortality to basic human warmth, she cries. Very probably Dell in this poem has revealed Millay's innermost thoughts.

When Millay could bear no more of Dell's probing into her psyche she ended the relationship, but their affair had not been without its share of spontaneous enjoyment. At times Millay was very coy with Dell. Frequently she took an inordinately long time in dressing for their dates. Millay established a pattern with him that she was to repeat in her subsequent affairs, at first being sweet and devoted, then increasingly irritable, and finally breaking off the relationship. After they were reconciled, which can be assumed from the last two lines of "Child of the lightning," she began the pattern again.[15]

From the beginning, the relationship of Edna St. Vincent Millay and Floyd Dell was probably ill fated. She needed an assertive, masculine, and intelligent man, but she did not want to have her freedom severely jeopardized. Dell's chattering, meddling, and attempting to psychoanalyze her no doubt taxed her patience, yet Dell was often helpful and kind. When Norma and Edna moved to the Village, Dell helped the two sisters find the apartment at 139 Waverly Place.

As a socialist and pacifist, Dell encouraged Millay to adopt his beliefs. Although Millay later developed a strong sense of social consciousness, she was not immediately influenced by Dell's socialism but shared his abhorrence of war. He was successful in urging Millay to become a more outspoken advocate of women's rights and perhaps influenced her concept of "free form" marriage, which she later shared with her husband. His supposed atheism probably influenced Millay to discard some conventional Christian ideas, but she always retained her deep love of mankind. Although Dell read and admired much of Millay's poetry, he did not substantially influence her style.

Floyd Dell made one highly significant contribution to the life and works of Edna St. Vincent Millay. He helped her to clarify her attitude toward women and to dispel the "bogeys which haunt the realm of grown-up man-woman love." Millay was deeply involved with the most profound emotions of man. Love, with all its nuances, was the ruling force of her life and works. Despite her resentment of Dell's constant probing, she nevertheless owed him a great debt for freeing her to write such fine work as *Twenty Sonnets,* which appeared in *Reedy's Mirror* in April and May of 1920 and which included "Into the golden vessel of great song," "Love is not blind, I see with single eye," "I pray you if you love me, bear my joy," and "And you as well must die, beloved dust." Floyd Dell dared to open the door into Millay's most intimate thoughts, but he did not profane her *hetaerae*; rather he presented her a glimpse of Phaon. Two years after Millay met Floyd Dell, she wrote:

> Let us go forth together to the spring
> Love must be this, if it be anything.

4

THIS ROOM WITHOUT FIRE:

Edmund Wilson

They talked of Catullus, Verlaine, and Dante and sipped peach brandy. She said how lovely the moon was, and he replied, "It looks like a bubble in the glass." When she began to read her poetry aloud, he forgot her shabby black dress and sharp nose and noticed instead her vibrant, flushed face and auburn hair. As dawn drew near, he wrapped her legs in a blanket and poured her more brandy. She filled the air with smoke and the ashtray with burnt-out cigarettes. As the sun rose in the damp, chilly air, he hailed her a taxi. She said she would like to go to the ballet on Tuesday. He had long admired her poetry, but he had only met her in the spring of 1920 at a party in Greenwich Village. She had told her escort that she wanted to go home alone, that she was an independent woman. Later Edna St. Vincent Millay had left the party with Edmund Wilson, who became another serious suitor in the Village. As Wilson returned to his apartment on Bank Street, with its Whistler print and large mahogany desk, he felt for the first time that literature was reality.[1]

Throughout his life, Edmund Wilson served as an intellectual stimulus for talented women. A personal friend of Elinor Wylie, Wilson lived in her apartment while she was away from

New York, and he sympathized with Millay when she resigned in anger from "the fusty province" of the League of American Penwomen, who had expelled Elinor Wylie in disapproval of her personal life. Shortly after Wilson married Mary McCarthy, his third wife, his irritation over her writing critical reviews instead of her own fiction became so intense that he locked her in a room several hours each day with a typewriter, telling her that she might do what she wished during this time. Finally, McCarthy yielded to both husband and muse and produced numerous fine novels, including *The Group*, based on her life at Vassar. Although Wilson did not attempt anything so dramatic with Millay, he found a publisher for her in *Vanity Fair* and steadily shaped the critical acclaim Millay so richly deserved.

Four years before Wilson drank bootleg gin with Millay at bohemian parties in the Village, he had read both "The Suicide" and "Interim" in copies of the *Vassar Miscellany Monthly* and *A Book of Vassar Verse*, which his cousin Caroline Wilson had given him in 1916. Then a cub reporter for the New York *Evening Sun*, Wilson published enthusiastic reviews of both poems, finding in them "a new note of frankness, intensity and dramatic feeling." A year later when Wilson was in the Army in France, Caroline sent him a copy of *Renascence*, which he treasured for the rest of his military stint.

When Wilson met Millay in the spring of 1920, she had abandoned hope of supporting herself by acting but had no real market for her poetry. From time to time she sold poetry to *Dial* and a few poems and her Nancy Boyd articles to *Ainslee's*, which Wilson with typical candor considered "trashy."[2] Using his position as assistant editor of *Vanity Fair*, a magazine catering to upper-class tastes, for romantic as well as artistic purposes Wilson urged Millay to sell her work to *Vanity Fair*, which would give her a wider and more literate audience. Curiously, Millay felt that she should also share her time and affection with another editor of *Vanity Fair*, John Peale Bishop, a situation that greatly annoyed Wilson. But sharing a place with Aldous Huxley, D. H. Lawrence, T. S. Eliot, and Ezra Pound in *Vanity Fair* certainly assured Millay more financial and popular success than she had enjoyed before.

In July 1920, *Vanity Fair* published Millay's poem "Dead Music—An Elegy" and for the next three years published most of her poetry and all of her Nancy Boyd articles. Frank Crowninshield, the fatherly editor, complained of the difficulty of having two of his assistants in love with one of his best contributors but was so pleased with Millay's work that he decided to send her to Europe to write more Nancy Boyd articles. Strongly encouraging Crowninshield to finance the trip, Wilson hoped that Millay would both broaden her artistic and cultural vistas and recover from "another small nervous breakdown." When she sailed on January 4, 1921, on the *Rochambeau*, she hoped to discover "fresh grass" for her poetry to feed on and to lose her feeling of artistic "sterility."[3]

Always maintaining his protective role, Wilson sometimes shielded Millay from Crowninshield's understandable irritation. On September 14, 1922, she wrote Wilson asking him not to let anyone cut her article "The Key" and not to let Crowninshield tamper with any work under her own name nor to sign her real name to her Nancy Boyd articles.[4] On May 2, 1923, she urged Wilson not to let "Crowny" be too angry with her for not having written any recent articles for *Vanity Fair*, because she was too "very tired and ill" to write at all.[5] Throughout her life, Millay had a cavalier attitude about business affairs that only someone as patient as Wilson could excuse. She was either notoriously late in answering letters or did not answer them at all; she left manuscripts strewn in apartments as she fled to the country or hid them so well that she might not find them until ten years later; her only draft of *Conversation at Midnight* was destroyed in a hotel fire; and she never finished her proposed novel *Hardigut* even though she had accepted a $500 advance. But Wilson soothed Crowninshield's ire sufficiently, and *Vanity Fair* resumed publication of Millay's work in 1928 after five year's silence.

Sharing deep artistic integrity, Millay and Wilson occasionally criticized each other's work. When she was sick in 1920, he typed dictation of her work, and in 1928 he met her at the Vanderbilt Hotel to discuss her bobolink poem. Although Millay was not offended by his portrait of her in *I Thought of Daisy*, she felt that the book was "uneven" and "not ready to be published" and wrote him copious notes about the novel, which he unfortunately did not receive until after her death.

One of the greatest debts that Millay owed Edmund Wilson was his attempt to secure for her the critical acclaim she deserved. Many critics were reluctant to acknowledge Millay's significance: Malcolm Cowley did not take her work seriously during her lifetime; Allen Tate and John Crowe Ransom have never properly appreciated her poetry. Yet Edmund Wilson boldly declared:

> Edna Millay seems to me one of the only poets writing in English in our time who have attained to anything like the stature of great literary figures in an age in which prose has predominated.

He felt that Millay had the same talent for "giving supreme expression to profoundly felt personal experience..." as Eliot, Auden, and Yeats.[6]

On a more personal level, Wilson offered Millay a relationship that was a rare blend of emotional and intellectual sharing. Several months after he met her, he formally proposed marriage to her in Jig Cook's house at Truro, near the tip of Cape Cod. She did not reject his proposal but said that she would think about it. Wilson wryly commented, "Proposals of marriage were not a source of great excitement."[7]

They went to a number of ballets, plays, concerts, and operas, especially enjoyed George Bernard Shaw's *Heartbreak House*, read scientific books together, and discussed the vision of human futility. When she was in Europe, Wilson sent her volumes of poetry, and he was keenly aware that "her poetry...was her real overmastering passion."

In addition to the intellectual aspect of their relationship, they also shared a spontaneous joy of life, which is captured in one of Millay's letters to Wilson:

> Bunny, I adored your drunken letter. Never be sober again, oh, lofty, one, O Centaur with song in his heart and burrs in his tail....I do solemnly offer this pious pagan prayer: That one of these days you'll become a dirty inveterate souse, and bully your wife and beat your kids and kick your dog, and think of me with steadfast love.[8]

In another letter, Millay enclosed a mock Chaucerian poem, exclaiming delight on receiving "A doulche billet from ye fatte Bunnye." In *I Thought of Daisy*, Wilson accepts Millay's various roles with understanding and humor:

> I had noted...in Rita [Edna Millay], the Irish fickle-mindedness and sharpness; the traces of the superior person in the small provincial community; of the bold and original personality in the community of college girls...; the intonations of the American actress of English light comedy; and, finally, dominating all, her role of princess and rake of the Village.

Again in *Daisy*, Wilson poignantly sums up his feelings for Millay:

> I should have asked nothing better of life than to have fitted up such a house, to have passed my days alone with Rita [Edna] in those high quiet rooms, hidden away among those crooked streets, with poetry and love!

Just as Edmund Wilson heightened Millay's intellectual awareness and supported her in times of emotional and physical stress, Millay was instrumental in freeing Wilson from the snobbery, repression, and coldness of his moneyed, distinguished family. Born three years earlier than Millay, Wilson was the product of prep schools, professional men—preachers, lawyers, and doctors—and domineering, aggressive women. During the time Millay was wandering the coast of Maine with her two equally uninhibited sisters, Wilson was being shuttled between Hill School in Pottstown, Pennsylvania, where his classmates taunted him incessantly with his childhood nickname, "Bunny," and for his bulbous nose, and his affluent home in Red Bank, New Jersey, where his mother berated his father for his "bookish" approach to life and Edmund, Jr., for his failure with athletics. While Cora Millay encouraged her daughters to be musical, artistic, and poetic, scoffed at domesticity per se, and gave them more than enough love to compensate for the lack of money, Helen Wilson lacked tact and sensitivity and was totally immersed in outward tokens of social appearance. When John Dos Passos, a lifelong friend of Wilson's, was imprisoned for participating in a protest over the poor working conditions of Kentucky coal miners, she merely said, "I see they've caught Dos Passos." Once Helen was quite disappointed when her husband arranged a trip to Europe when she had hoped to go to Florida, which she considered more fashionable. The disciplinarian of the family, Mrs. Wilson spanked her only child with a silver-backed brush and generally monopolized and dominated him.

Most of the love and warmth that Wilson enjoyed as a child radiated from his father, Edmund Wilson, Sr., a brilliant trial lawyer, who at various times was the attorney for the Pennsylvania Railroad, a member of the New Jersey Board of Railroad Commissioners, and the Attorney General of New Jersey. Despite his successful career, Wilson, Sr., had an essential humanity and often spoke to Negro audiences, being a sincere admirer of Booker T. Washington, and as his son noted, "completely without snobbery of race or class." Sadly, Wilson, Sr., became bored with his early success, and when he was thirty-five began to suffer from "neurotic eclipses," accompanied by acute depression, that left him confined to sanitariums or at home in a room with a felt-covered door for the last thirty years of his life. Wilson's fear of inheriting his father's melancholia is reflected in the depression of the narrator in *Ellen Terhune* and *I Thought of Daisy* and became reality when he had a nervous breakdown in his middle thirties.

Whereas Millay found the social restrictions almost intoler-able at Vassar, Wilson discovered a more catholic view of life at Princeton. Especially in his professor, Christian Gauss, Wilson found a warm and genuine father figure, who read Wilson's manuscripts, corresponded with him until his death, invited him to his home, and instilled in him a conviction of the "morality" of literature. Competent, human, and a lover of literature and theater, Gauss served as an important "spiritual and intellectual force"[9] throughout Wilson's life.

When Wilson met Millay in the spring of 1920, he was in the process of overcoming the limited vision of people caused by his exclusive background. Despite his friendship with Gauss, most of the Princeton undergraduates had regarded Edmund Wilson, Jr., as "a withdrawn, literary figure, a well-dressed...grind, a smug, conceited little fellow."[10] Wilson was unable "to engage with life, to experience it at first hand."[11] But his experiences in World War II did much to acquaint him with a wide range of people:

> I could never go back to my former life....My experience of the army had had on me a liberating effect. I could now get on with all kinds of people and could satisfy my curiosity about aspects of life that otherwise I should not perhaps so soon have known.[12]

When F. Scott Fitzgerald, a close friend of Wilson's at Princeton, saw him in 1920 in New York he said that he "was no longer the shy little scholar of Holder Court—he walked with confidence....There was something else that was nourishing him...the Metropolitan Spirit...."[13] Millay played a definite part in Wilson's new sense of freedom. The day after he met her he mused, "Now the Village was at last revealed to me; it had that day come alive about me, and I felt myself part of its life."[14] In *This Room and This Gin and These Sandwiches*, Tracy, the stage manager, says of Sally (Edna Millay) and Arthur (Edmund Wilson): "She's loosened him up; he's more human than he was."

Today Edmund Wilson is considered one of the most influential and vigorous critics of the twentieth century, having written numerous articles, two novels, one volume of plays, and seventeen book-length critical works. Significantly, he treats Edna St. Vincent Millay in four works—his play *This Room and This Gin and These Sandwiches*, both of his novels, *I Thought of Daisy* and *Memoirs of Hecate County*, and the epilogue to *The Shores of Light*—which shed light on their relationship and his actual influence on her works and personality.

Although *This Room and This Gin and These Sandwiches* was first published in 1937 under its original title *A Winter in Beech Street,* the events and spirit of the play clearly stem from Wilson's Greenwich Village days. The Beech Street Players obviously represent the Provincetown Players, who produced Wilson's first play, *The Crime in the Whistler Room*, in October 1924. Both the Beech Street Playhouse and the Provincetown Playhouse are located at 18 Macdougal Street, where actors and journalists discuss the *Masses*, which "Nobody but the radicals" write for, and the Payson (Paterson) Strike.

In *This Room and This Gin and These Sandwiches*, Arthur Fiske, a reserved architect, is based on Edmund Wilson while Sally Voight, a pretty, neurotic actress, is modeled on Edna Millay (Sherman Paul, however, suggests that Mary Blair, Wilson's first wife, might have been Sally). Wearing "the dress of the young Eastern college graduate who continues to dress like an undergraduate" and commenting, "I suddenly realized then that I couldn't go back to the way I'd lived," Arthur clearly reflects Wilson's Princeton days and his stint in the army. When Arthur says to Sally, "*You* represent the only morality that I can care anything about. The only real morality and the only real beauty," he echoes Wilson's beliefs in *Daisy* that literature is reality and that moral values are aesthetic values. Most importantly, Arthur is the only person in the play with a firm grip on reality.

Trying to seek her fortune as an actress with the Beech Street Players, just as Millay did with the Provincetown Players, Sally is a small woman with an air of independence: "I don't want to live with anybody. I want to be myself." Throughout the play, Sally rebuffs Arthur's incessant proposals of marriage, once taunting him with, "Yes: I'll think about it." Like Millay, Sally has financial problems, which Arthur remedies by paying her overdue rent and part of her abortion costs. Above Sally's bed there is "a large modern painting, in which erotic and fleshy female contours seem to be combined with machinery—*Directions for Using the Empress*," just as a Charles Ellis' (Norma's husband) painting hung in Millay's bedroom in the Village—"A modern painting, all fractured geometrical planes that vaguely delineated a female figure," which the sisters called *Directions for Using the Empress*. Just as Sally and Tracy sing of careless love and cocaine, the Millay sisters sang folk songs about cocaine[15] and darling men, whom they loved so long or "only a little while."[16]

At the center of *This Room* lies a power struggle within the Beech Street Players, climaxing in the company's dispute over which play to produce—*Lysistrata, Uncle Tom's Cabin*, or the perpetually drunken Fred's masterpiece, *Don Juan Comes to Bethelehem*. The subplot of the play concerns the romantic triangle of Arthur, Sally, and Bugs Broply, a charming but irresponsible newspaperman. Arthur is in love with

Sally, who is in love with Bugs, who is really too immature to love anyone but himself, telling Sally that his wife doesn't "believe" in him. When Sally becomes pregnant by Bugs and has a painful abortion, she maintains an unruffled facade but later bursts into tears, "It's horrible for me, too!—all these abortions and mutilations."

Throughout Sally's misfortunes, Arthur assumes a protective and supportive attitude toward her without seriously condemning her. After arranging and paying for her abortion, he comforts her after the operation, is concerned that she has lost so much blood, and offers to take her to lunch at the Breevort. He also cleans and redecorates her apartment, starting a fire and buying her a coal scuttle, poker, and tongs, making her untidy bed into a sofa, and replacing messy shelves with a china closet. Sally concedes, "You flatter my defects—Sometimes I love you very much." Appreciative of his kindness, Sally is still unable to make a total commitment to him, not only refusing to marry him, but also balking at the idea of living with him: "I've tried it, and you just bust up quicker that way." Feeling that monogamy would stifle their relationship, Sally says, "Love ought to be all meetings and partings—partings as much as meetings." At times Arthur defeats his own suit by jealously nagging her about other suitors, driving her to exclaim, "You make me feel so guilty all the time!—I'm fond of you, you know that—but you don't own me!" Seeming younger and less experienced than Sally throughout the play, Arthur reflects Wilson's statement in *The Shores of Light*: "At that time I was too young and too much in love to understand her well...."

Despite fears and jealousies, Arthur and Sally can share the magic of hurdy-gurdy men and nightingales. Early in the play Arthur tells Sally, "I used to lie awake at night in that hospital in the Vosges, and there would be nightingales singing outside, but I couldn't really hear them. I couldn't on account of the War." But later in the Village, he hears the hurdy-gurdy distinctly "and it seems to me perfectly marvelous!" Sally confides to Arthur, "You've given me something that nobody else has—you've given me a kind of repose. But people have to fight against relaxing." Ironically, Sally cannot hear the hurdy-gurdy man "because something that was here has gone." But the beauty of their relationship lies in the gifts exchanged—peace to Sally and *joie de vivre* to Arthur.

Again in *Ellen Terhune*, Edmund Wilson composes a variation on the theme of Edna Millay's life, exploring in even greater depth and sensitivity their delicate spiritual and emotional bond. Early in the story, striking similarities between Ellen Terhune and Edna Millay are presented. Both women are artists with a "non-fashionable character" about their work—in an age of the twelve-tone scale, Ellen writes classical sonatas, whereas Edna wrote sonnets when free verse was enjoying great popularity. Edna, of course, was also a pianist. A small, green-eyed woman, Ellen usually goes to Maine or Nantucket for the summer, reminiscent of Millay's childhood in Maine and love of the seashore. Ellen has married too late to have children, while Edna married at thirty, an age when many women do not bear their first child. Sherman Paul considers Ellen's home, the ornate, sprawling Vallambrosa, an inversion of Millay's simple, tasteful, and beautifully landscaped Steepletop.[17]

As *Ellen Terhune* opens, the narrator (Wilson) visits Ellen, whose emotional disturbance has checked her creative ability. After a few drinks and cigarettes, Ellen plays her depressing four-note second movement of a sonata, which falls short of the traditional slow, subdued second movement in having no real development or variation. Finding the work boring, inexpressive, and a little insane, the narrator nevertheless gives Ellen superficial praise and advice about her music. The supernatural elements of the story—on successive visits, the narrator sees Ellen in two earlier stages of her life and her mother as a young woman—intensify the probing Jamesian tone.

Torn between steadfast devotion to music and neurotic

need for love and understanding, Ellen Terhune presents more of a challenge than the narrator can meet. Aware of the more confident, aggressive facet of Ellen's personality, he notes that she was "the kind of self-managing woman that it is hard to do anything for" and a "self-confident woman... who knows that she can compete with men in fields which they have largely monopolized...." But her thirst for human warmth, symbolized by her epileptic seizures and nervous headaches, cannot be satiated by her love of music or relationship with the narrator, who himself has "certain neurotic states," occasional depressions, and fleeting suicidal urges. Near the end of the story, Ellen's revision of the second movement reveals the depth of her tortured soul:

> This cry [of the music], itself now reiterated, not only wrecked the bounds of the conventional, it seemed even to escape from the probable—anguished, appealing, pitying, recognizing all human discrepancy, debasement, self-disgust and self-accusal of the individual who knows his own nature and who yet cannot undo what he is....

But as the music ends (in the illusionary Jamesian framework) and as Ellen dies (in reality, far from Vallambrosa, in a decaying New York hotel),

> The voice broke away: for that moment, becoming at once more complex and more ordered, it had been freed to a life of its own....

Unable to find solace in the narrator's flowers, notes, and frequent visits, Ellen Terhune escapes through "the peace of the grave / And the light of the sun."

Sherman Paul views *Ellen Terhune* as a "confession of guilt and an act of atonement, a story by means of which Wilson tries to right his relations with Edna Millay."[18] But the narrator fails Ellen only in his inability to have delicate and perfect communication, by always maintaining a facade of detachment, which masks his deep and genuine concern for the young woman. To break through this barrier, Wilson could have tried Floyd Dell's type of meddling, which Millay resented. Instead, Wilson retained an air of objectivity, made necessary by Millay's neurosis. *Ellen Terhune* reflects Wilson's respect and concern for Millay and her trust in him, but at this time she could not surrender completely to another person.

In commemoration of her first meeting with Edmund Wilson, when they talked of poetry and sipped peach brandy, Millay wrote "Portrait," first published in the *Saturday Review of Literature* in 1928. Wilson later wrote, "It is painful to me to reread this poem today and to feel again, in retrospect, how much I must have hated to part from her."[19]

In the first stanza of "Portrait," Millay celebrates "the terrible weight of the perfect word" as Wilson reads aloud to her with a "voice harsh and light" as they share "illustrious living and dead" and "immortal page after page conceived in mortal mind":

> Over and over I have heard,
> As now I hear it,
> Your voice harsh and light as the scratching of dry
>   leaves over the hard ground,
> Your voice forever assailed and shaken by the wind
>   from the island
> Of illustrious living and dead, that never dies down,
> And bending at moments under the terrible weight of
>   the perfect word....

The beauty and reality of literature, "a wild bright bird," triumph over physical discomforts of "this room without fire," just as the narrator in *Daisy* covers Rita's legs with a blanket as the night grows cold:

> Here in this room without fire, without comfort of any kind,
> Reading aloud to me immortal page after page conceived in a
>   mortal mind.

> Beauty at such moments before me like a wild bright bird
> Has been in the room, and eyed me, and let me come near it.

In the second stanza, the value of sharing literature becomes more personal to Millay, as the hours bring her rapture and peaceful comfort:

> I could not ever nor can I to this day
> Acquaint you with the triumph and the sweet rest
> These hours have brought to me and always bring,—
> Rapture coloured like the wild bird's neck and wing,
> Comfort, softer than the feathers of its breast.

Using bird imagery, Millay feels rapture, "coloured like the wild bird's neck and wing...." They share flight—flight of the imagination, created by the reality of literature, and flight of the emotions in sharing literature with another sensitive person. They also share the "comfort" of human warmth, "softer than the feathers of its breast."

In the final stanza of "Portrait," Millay explores only her personal relationship with Wilson, being distraught over a lack of communication. When she tries "to tell you what I would have you know...," he scourges her with a salty flail:

> Always, and even now, when I rise to go,
> Your eyes blaze out from a face gone wickedly pale;
> I try to tell you what I would have you know,—
> What peace it was; you cry me down; you scourge me
>   with a salty flail;
> You will not have it so.

In "Portrait," Millay suggests that she and Wilson shared a nearly perfect intellectual communication, but that neither could achieve total, intimate emotional rapport.

Thus, regret over imperfect rapport in *Ellen Terhune* is mirrored in "Portrait." Probably any man would have had difficulty understanding Millay's complex, and sometimes neurotic, personality. But despite his own relative immaturity, inexperience, and personal crises—the search for a father, lack of *joie de vivre*, and fear of mental "eclipses"—Edmund

Wilson supported and protected the poet in many physical, emotional, and professional problems.

In *I Thought of Daisy* and *The Shores of Light*, Wilson is always modest about his influence on Millay, but he reveals that he gave her a much needed market for her work, occasionally criticized her work, secured for her the critical acclaim she so deserved, and offered her a relationship balancing love with intellect—a seemingly perfect combination for both Millay and Wilson. Sadly, Millay was not ready for a long-term union or marriage.

But there was always a strong bond between these two artists. Four years before her death, Millay wrote her friend: "But I think, and I think it often...'Some day I shall see him again, and we shall talk about poetry, as we used to do.' "[20] The night of October 20, 1950, Edmund Wilson dreamed of Millay in the Village and their conversation about John Peale Bishop's poetry. Unknown to Wilson, Millay had died the day before.[21] Not only were Edna St. Vincent Millay and Edmund Wilson joined by a conviction of "the terrible weight of the perfect word," they also basked in the warmth of the room without fire.

5

INTO THE GOLDEN VESSEL
OF GREAT SONG:

Arthur Davison Ficke

One winter night in 1918, a tall army major with dark wavy hair, blue eyes, and a finely chiseled nose hurried into New York carrying some important dispatches from Washington to General Pershing. Dropping in on Floyd Dell, his longtime friend from both Davenport and Chicago, the handsome officer asked Dell if he might meet Edna St.Vincet Millay, his poet-correspondent for the past six years. After a brisk walk to 139 Waverly Place, Dell introduced Arthur Davison Ficke to Norma Millay, her future husband Charles Ellis, and Edna St. Vincent Millay, who was immediately struck by Ficke's patrician beauty, witty conversation, and ability to listen. Leaving the guest of honor with the pretty Millay sisters, Dell and Ellis went to a local delicatessen for sandwiches and pickles and perhaps some bootleg gin. Later the tiny one-room apartment resounded with laughter and chatter as the Village bohemians sat on the floor enjoying their indoor picnic. As Norma grasped a huge pickle, she exclaimed, "This pickle is a little loving cup," which prompted Ficke to write the next morning:

> This pickle is a little loving cup,
> I raise it to my lips, and where you kissed

> There lurks a certain sting that I have missed
> In nectars more laboriously put up.[1]

Even though he was still married to Evelyn Blunt, Millay had an intense three-day affair with Ficke, who immediately began writing love sonnets to his "Spiritual Advisee." Of all her Village suitors, Ficke kindled in Millay the most desperate, futile, romantic love.

Six years earlier, on Thanksgiving Day 1912, Arthur Davison Ficke and Witter Bynner were leafing through Ficke's advance copy of *The Lyric Year* when they spotted Edna St. Vincent Millay's "Renascence," which Bynner immediately read to his host. Amazed by the poem and outraged that it had only won fourth place in the contest, the two men sat down at the base of the Soldier's Monument in Davenport, Iowa, and wrote Millay, "This is Thanksgiving Day and we thank you...." On December 5, 1912, Millay responded to the letter from Ficke, Bynner, and Evelyn Ficke, who had also signed the letter: "You are three dear people. This is Thanksgiving Day, too, and I thank you,"[2] thus beginning a lively and warm correspondence between Millay and Ficke, whom she one year later called her "Dear Spiritual Advisor."[3]

From the beginning the correspondence between Millay and Ficke was very human and spontaneous, as she frequently discussed her poetry and professional matters with him. On December 15, 1912, she wrote him concerning "Renascence," "As to the line you speak of—'Did you get it from a book?' Indeed! I'll slap your face. I never get anything from a book." She commented on the creation of "Renascence":

> I did see it, yes. I saw it all, more vividly than you may suppose. It was almost an experience....All of my poems are very real to me, and take a great deal out of me. I am possessed of a masterful and often a cruel imagination. All of this is just the wee-est bit confidential....[4]

In December 1912, Ficke sent Millay a book of William Blake, which she treasured the rest of her life. Later that month, she wrote Ficke that she had received a letter from a "lunatic" who had asked her to autograph the one hundred and eighty-eighth page of *The Lyric Year*, which contained her "Renascence." With refreshing honesty, Millay exclaimed, "I never got a letter just like it before. Is it usual? Do be indulgent and explain."[5]

By April 12, 1913, Millay referred to Ficke as her "Spiritual Advisor," being highly impressed with his "beautiful, beautiful book" *Twelve Japanese Painters* and feeling "drunk at this moment" with one section of the book, "The Birds and Flowers of Hiroshige."[6] During the next five years, Millay reported many amusing details and impressions of her life to her "advisor" in Davenport, Iowa. When she was attending Barnard College, she wrote Ficke, "I am learning Russian. There are one hundred copecks in one rouble, and Anna Karenina isn't pronounced that way."[7] Before she entered Vassar, Millay asked Ficke, "Aren't you going to send me a snap of *Her* and *It* [Ficke's wife and child]?" More seriously, she confided that "Andrew Marvel is an old love of mine..." and that Witter Bynner ruined his poem "Union Square" when he revised it. Ficke read of Millay's initial disgust with Vassar, a "pink-and-gray college," where the girls were trusted with everything but men. After discovering that Ficke had visited Poughkeepsie without seeing her, she wrote, "The thought that I was probably not here at the time does not lessen my grief, or my annoyance."

Although Ficke was nine years Millay's senior, she did not regard him as a father figure, as she later did her husband, except in the early correspondence when she considered him her "Spiritual Advisor." Instead, a sea of beauty, truth, and art moved between their souls. By the time Ficke met Millay, he was trying to solve two major problems common to many artistic personalities—the conflict between a more usual profession and complete dedication to art and the search for an intimate companion sensitive to the needs and desires of a creative person.

Just as Millay at times felt thwarted by her Nancy Boyd pieces and her acting career, Ficke resented the obligations of his legal career, which sapped his creative urge and love of Japanese prints. His father, Charles Augustus Ficke, a wealthy and successful lawyer, had decided that his son should pursue a legal career and sent him to Harvard in 1900. After receiving his B.A. in 1904, Ficke traveled around the world with his parents for a year, spent two years as a law student and English instructor at the State University of Iowa, then passed the Iowa Bar in 1908, and practiced law with his father in Davenport until 1917. After nine years in Davenport Ficke became bored and frustrated with the seemingly empty ritual of his life, which he escaped by frequent trips to Chicago, where he revelled in sales of Japanese prints, which he had loved from an early age, the theater, the Art Institute, and visits with Floyd Dell.

In 1917 Ficke entered World War I as a captain, an appointment made possible by the influence of his father-in-law and his own legal competency,[8] although Ficke later said, "Probably there is no one alive who is less of a real soldier than I am."[9] Nevertheless, when he met Edna Millay he had become a major and was appointed a lieutenant colonel shortly before his honorable dismissal. In much the same way that war experience enhanced Edmund Wilson's appreciation of a wide range of people, the army increased Ficke's sense of self-confidence. Returning to Davenport in 1919, Ficke was determined to leave his father's law firm and went to his office and began to talk with him in a general way, leading up to the subject of his quitting the legal profession. Midway through the talk, Charles Augustus Ficke abruptly said, "Arthur, you've smoked enough." Ficke replied with quiet sarcasm, "After more than two years in the American Army,

finally with the responsibilities of a lieutenant colonel, I
think I may be permitted to decide how many cigarettes I
may smoke." Arthur Davison Ficke was then free to write his
Hymn to Intellectual Beauty.[10]

By the end of the war, Ficke was beginning to realize the
folly of his ten-year marriage to Evelyn Blunt, the daughter
of an army general, whose military background encouraged in
her a certain reserve and coldness.[11] When Arthur and Witter
Bynner had conceived the *Spectra* hoax in 1916, Evelyn was
so annoyed by their wild laughter and general foolishness
that she ordered them out of the house until they had finished their manuscript.[12] During the war, Ficke had met two
women who more fully satisfied his intellectual and emotional needs—Edna St. Vincent Millay and Gladys Brown. His
romantic interlude with Millay in Greenwich Village had
inspired him to write many love sonnets. In France he met
Gladys Brown,[13] a pretty, intelligent, and sympathetic artist,
who perhaps even more than Millay helped Arthur clarify his
feeling toward Evelyn Blunt. Yet Ficke was hesitant to
divorce his wife during the war because she was chronically
ill.

Arthur Davison Ficke's impact on Edna Millay cannot be
easily measured. Jean Gould says, "To Edna St. Vincent Millay...the light-hearted evening was a soul-shaking event: for
the first time in her life she found herself falling in love. It
was a miraculous yet terrifying sensation...she was powerless
to stem her emotions." Miriam Gurko believes that Millay fell
in love with Ficke the night she met him and that "the
encounter, though brief, was long enough to touch them
both with an intense emotion." Norman Brittin comments,
"The flaming of their passion, the quick consummation of
love, and their being wrenched apart so violently constituted
a devastating experience." Elizabeth Atkins does not even
comment on the relationship between Millay and Ficke.

Certainly Millay's "powerless" love for Ficke is an exagger-

ation. Millay never lost control of her emotions or her creative ability, except perhaps through her illnesses—migraine
headaches, spinal trouble,[14] nervous breakdowns—which
became increasingly oppressive during the last twenty years
of her life. But Millay's "intense emotion" certainly smol-
dered in her letters to Ficke after their brief union. In October 1921, she wrote him, "My time, in those awful days after
you went away to France, was a mist of thinking about you
& writing sonnets to you."[15] In her most moving love letter
to Ficke, Millay revealed the depth of her involvement:

> I love you, too, my dear, and shall always, just as I did the first
> moment I saw you. You are a part of Loveliness to me....It
> doesn't matter at all that we never see each other, & that we
> write so seldom. We shall never escape from each other....It [our
> love] is a thing that exists, simply, like a sapphire, like anything
> roundly beautiful; there is nothing to be done about it,—&
> nothing one would wish to do....You will never grow old to me,
> or die, or be lost in any way.[16]

Millay was attracted by Ficke's physical beauty, wit, and
intelligence, but her love for him was not merely based on his
"blinding impact of physical beauty": for six years she had
been discovering facets of his personality through his letters.
In 1915 Millay wrote, "Think of this:—you may have told me
a hundred things that you fancy still secreted in your esoteric
heart!—Doesn't that make you awfully nervous?"

In 1937 Millay painfully recalled how "terribly...sick-
eningly" in love with Ficke she had been years before.
But Millay had a penchant for exaggeration, which Edmund
Wilson noted in *The Shores of Light*, "There was something
of awful drama about everything one did with Edna." Millay
was also capable, as are many fine poets, of pushing her emotions to the limit in order to provide the inspiration for
poetry, or as Wilson crystallized it in *I Thought of Daisy*, "It
was as if, in their contacts with Rita [Edna], they [her
friends] had become somehow facets of herself, their

longings given body by her force. They had become aspects of her own personality...." Millay felt deeply about Ficke, but she probably did not suffer from unrequited love for the rest of her life.

Ficke's very inaccessibility made him even more attractive to Millay, as Witter Bynner wrote, "She was not so romantically in love with me as she had been from the first with Arthur—perhaps because he was married and more difficult to attain...."[17] A frantic union of only three days heightened Ficke's romantic appeal for Millay, but she was not being totally honest when she wrote him, "It doesn't matter at all that we never see each other and that we write so seldom," for later in the same letter she admitted: "One's body, too, is so lonely." But from an artistic standpoint, the separation produced the vital tension for the creation of such sonnets as "Into the golden vessel of great song" and "And you as well must die, beloved dust." During her separation from Ficke, Millay was also involved in highly meaningful relationships with Floyd Dell, Edmund Wilson, and Eugen Boissevain. She also felt that she could love two men at the same time, as is revealed in a letter to Ficke: "Well, there's no denying that I love you, my dear....But that's no reason why I couldn't marry Hal [Witter Bynner], and be happy with him. I love him, too. In a different way."

Although Millay probably intensified her love for Ficke in order to write more vivid poetry, she nevertheless cherished a real love for him. More handsome than Floyd Dell and Edmund Wilson, Arthur Davison Ficke also had an aura of self-confidence, which no doubt impressed Millay, who was nine years younger than he. (Even though Ficke had not, in 1918, made the final break with his father, his wife, or his legal practice, the army was already having a positive effect on his self-concept.) Millay shared a real intellectual rapport with Ficke, as with Wilson, admitting to him in 1913, "I have yet to learn the ABC's of my art," after which she freely discussed her work with Ficke.

During 1919 and 1920, Ficke's letters to Millay were much cooler in tone than those written after their first meeting in 1918. Instead of declarations of love, he irately asked her to return some sonnets he had sent her. Disappointed that Arthur had embarked on a trip to the Orient with Bynner rather than returning to New York to resume their love affair, Millay maintained a cheerful facade in letters to both men, but at times loneliness seeped through the mask of cheerful insouciance. After gaily berating Bynner with "When are you two boys coming back here?" she admitted, "I miss you like hell." Perhaps regretting her transient relationship with Arthur, she added to her request for a kimono, "And don't go scorning my childish request just because I don't happen to be your idiot cousin or your divorced wife or somebody else with a rightful claim." During this time her deep involvement with Edmund Wilson had culminated in his marriage proposal, but her general melancholy and blasé attitude kept her from being very interested in the proposal.

The main reason for the breakup of Millay and Ficke was his involvement with Gladys Brown, whom he had met shortly after he arrived in France, where she was an ambulance driver with a group organized by the Women's Suffrage Party. Gladys was not especially interested in poetry then, but she agreed to meet Ficke because he was supposed to be handsome.[18] Apparently the young painter made quite an impression on Ficke, because he did not see Millay again until 1922, when he introduced Gladys to Millay at Prunier's in Paris,[19] a meeting that caused Millay both joy for Ficke and regret for things past, as is revealed in her letter to Ficke: "Isn't it funny about you & Gladys?—My God—it's marvelous....And you didn't think we'd like each other!—men don't know very much....I shall love you till the day I die...." During the four years of their separation, while she was supposedly grieving over Ficke, Millay was being courted by Wil-

son, Dell, and Boissevain, and Ficke was pursuing Gladys
Brown. In late 1919 or early 1920, Gladys Brown, dressed in
a luscious blue satin gown, attended a ball in New York but
was totally unaware that Ficke was present too. When they
accidentally met on the stairs, Arthur delightedly exclaimed,
"Well, there is dirty little Gladys"—a nickname he had given
her in France because she was often stained with grease and
oil from the ambulance she drove for the Women's Overseas
Hospital. They corresponded frequently after that meeting,
but Arthur could not make the final decision to leave Evelyn
Blunt, who was very sick.

Finally in 1923, Ficke came to New York, had an all-night
talk with Gladys, and told her that she had a "talent for
love." A spunky woman, she made her position clear: she
would marry him, live with him unmarried, or they could
maintain separate residences in different cities, but she would
not share him with another woman. At that time, Ficke
decided to get a divorce, Gladys lived with Arthur until the
divorce was final, and they were married in 1924 in Edna and
Eugen Boissevain's Bedford Street house in New York.[20]

Edna St. Vincent Millay and Arthur Davison Ficke were
not destined to have a lifelong romantic involvement.
Although Ficke understood Millay's poetry, served as an
inspiration for her sonnets, and was a rare blend of the emotional and the intellectual, she might well have been disappointed with this man, whom she had idealized to godlike
proportions, had she lived with him for any length of time.
Marriages of highly creative people are often not successful.
Although the Brownings seemed to have enjoyed an idyllic
relationship, Scott Fitzgerald's alcoholism and Zelda's insanity reciprocally weakened both writers. Arthur and Edna
might well have suffered from professional jealousy, disputes
over whose career was to take precedence, a lack of stability
in both, and an overall decline in the creative efforts of both
poets. Admiring both Edna Millay and Gladys Brown for

their beauty and talent, Ficke perhaps found in Gladys more sympathy and stability than in Edna, who was becoming increasingly neurotic. Yet the first meeting of Millay and Ficke remains important for the poetry they both wrote.

Ficke probably had more influence on the form of Millay's poetry and her mature theme of the permanence of love than any of her other suitors in the Village. Since his first edition of *Sonnets of a Portrait-Painter* appeared in 1914, Millay probably read the volume before she started producing her best sonnets in Greenwich Village. In defiance of popular taste, Ficke wrote sonnets, which contained classical references, some of which even foreshadow specific lines of Millay's poetry. The syntax of Ficke's lyrics "The Potter" and "The Tidings" is later echoed in Millay's "Dirge Without Music." The terse sentences in Ficke's "The Potter," "Then go, I do not want you. It is over..." and again in "The Tidings," "Life wanes. The sunlight darkens. You are dead..." are brought to the fullest development in "Dirge Without Music," "I know. But I do not approve. And I am not resigned." There is marked similarity between the themes and phrasing of Ficke's "Possession," "Yesterday you were mine, beloved and fair. / Today I seek, another love is there..." and Millay's bitter sonnet to meddlesome men such as Floyd Dell, "Bluebeard," "That I must never more behold your face. / This now is yours. I seek another place."

After Millay left Greenwich Village, she continued to respect Ficke's critical abilities. Shortly after Gladys and Arthur Ficke arrived in Santa Fe, New Mexico, in 1926, they asked the "Millay-Boissevains" to visit them and sent them traveling expenses. Millay brought with her the manuscript of *The King's Henchman*, the libretto for Deems Taylor's opera, and asked Arthur's help in a complete revision, which they worked on furiously during the three-week visit, and Millay left with an essentially new libretto. Both Arthur and Gladys were surprised by this incident, since Millay rarely asked for or accepted significant criticism of her work. During this visit, the Fickes and Boissevains also pursued the less literary activity of photographing each other in the nude. Ficke took a number of nude pictures of Edna and Gladys, some of them highly artistic dance poses. A memorable picture from this visit, in the Dadaist vein, shows both couples, scantily dressed, sipping drinks around a table.[21]

Impassioned by her meeting with Arthur Davison Ficke, Millay wrote a number of sonnets, including "There is no shelter in you anywhere," "Into the golden vessel of great song," and "And you as well must die, beloved dust"; all three were included in the series of twenty sonnets published in *Reedy's Mirror* in the spring of 1920. "Into the golden vessel of great song" and "And you as well must die, beloved dust" later appeared in the first edition of *Second April* in 1921, but "There is no shelter in you anywhere" was never included in a volume of Millay's poetry. In 1921, Millay wrote Ficke that both "Into the golden vessel of great song" and "There is no shelter in you anywhere" were written to him, but denied having written "And you as well must die, beloved dust" to Ficke until 1945. Later that year, in Hillsdale, New York, Millay read "beloved dust" and portions from *Lycidas* at Ficke's funeral.

In "There is no shelter in you anywhere," Millay celebrates her strong, yet painful, love and passion for Ficke:

> I only know that every hour with you
> Is torture to me, and that I would be
> From your too poignant lovelinesses free!

Love is unbearably beautiful, engaging all the senses, until together beauty and pain flood and then ebb:

> Rainbows, green flame, sharp diamonds, the fierce blue
> Of shimmering ice-bergs, and to be shot through
> With lightning or a sword incessantly—
> Such things have beauty, doubtless; but to me
> Mist, shadow, silence—these are lovely too.

As the pain of love becomes more intense, Millay feels exposed and helpless:

> There is no shelter in you anywhere;
> Rhythmic, intolerable, your burning rays
> Trample upon me, withering my breath.

Feeling her independence threatened and dreading the death of love, Millay decides to withdraw from the love affair:

> I will be gone, and rid of you, I swear:
> To stand upon the peaks of Love always
> Proves but that part of Love whose name is Death.

"Into the golden vessel of great song" represents an attempt to intellectualize love, or to sublimate passion.[22] Instead of accepting love with tranquility, Millay and Ficke pour all their passion "Into the golden vessel of great song":

> Into the golden vessel of great song
> Let us pour all our passion; breast to breast
> Let other lovers lie, in love and rest....

By expressing their love in words and song, they will merge both physical and intellectual love into the "common soul":

> Not we,—articulate, so, but with the tongue
> Of all the world: the churning blood, the long
> Shuddering quiet, the desperate hot palms pressed
> Sharply together upon the escaping guest,
> The common soul, unguarded, and grown strong.

Unwilling for their love to become as commonplace as fruit fallen on the ground, the two lovers will exalt their love with music of singers and minstrels:

> Longing alone is singer to the lute;
> Let still on nettles in the open sigh
> The minstrel, that in slumber is as mute
> As any man, and love be far and high,
> That else forsakes the topmost branch, a fruit
> Found on the ground by every passer-by.

"And you as well must die, beloved dust" is a bitter indictment of death, which carelessly destroys physical beauty—a theme that recurs in "Dirge Without Music." In this sonnet, Millay does not seek escape from love or comfort in intellectualized passion, rather she bemoans the loss of physical beauty:

> And you as well must die, beloved dust,
> And all your beauty stand you in no stead;
> This flawless, vital hand, this perfect head,
> This body of flame and steel, before the gust
> Of Death, or under his autumnal frost,
> Shall be as any leaf, be no less dead
> Than the first leaf that fell,—this wonder fled,
> Altered, estranged, disintegrated, lost.

Not only will death try to end physical love, but death will also attempt to check spiritual love:

> Nor shall my love avail you in your hour.
> In spite of all my love, you will arise
> Upon that day and wander down the air
> Obscurely as the unattended flower,
> It mattering not how beautiful you were,
> Or how beloved above all else that dies.

Although Millay momentarily hopes that Ficke will undergo a pantheistic rebirth like the "unattended flower," she finally berates death for its thoughtless destruction of beauty and love.

Millay's three sonnets to Ficke reveal a development in her attitude toward both her "Spiritual Advisor" and the nature of love itself. In "There is no shelter in you anywhere," Millay is so awed by the beauty and pain of love that she sees no solution but flight to a neutral peace. "Into the golden vessel of great song" shows Millay willing to accept love, with all its beauty and pain, but through intellectualized passion. In the final sonnet, Millay embraces all nuances of love—pain, beauty, death, and selflessness—climaxing in her barbs at death for its uncaring devastation of her "beloved dust," her most mature view of love until much later in the Village.

Despite Ficke's supposed indifference to Millay, he nevertheless replied to her love poems with a sequence of seventeen sonnets, *A Hymn to Intellectual Beauty*, in 1922, changing the title in 1926 to *Beauty in Exile*. Throughout the sequence, Ficke traces the growth of his love for Millay through pure sensuality, deep spirituality, and tragic finality of life and love. In the first three sonnets, Ficke extols their purely sensual love, perhaps in memory of their brief union in New York. When Ficke first sees Millay, "a naked goddess at her bath," he is smitten blind as Tiresias to earthly, mundane concerns:

> Blind to the common and decaying things
> Blind to the dying summer and the dust,
> Blind to the crumpled wall, the broken wings,
> The yellow leaf, the sword ruined with rust;
> Blind, blind to all save the wild memory
> Of Beauty naked against a stormy sky.(I)

Millay becomes an earth goddess, touched by Beauty in early youth:

> For Beauty kissed your lips when they were young
> And touched them with Her fatal triumphing,
> And Her old tune that long ago was sung
> Beside your cradle haunts you when you sing. (II)

Both intellectual and physical beauty alienate her from the reality of worldly cares:

> You are an exile to those lonely lands
> Far out upon the world's forsaken rim
> Where there is never touch of meeting hands,—
> Always you must go on, through spaces dim,
> Seeking a refuge you can never know—
> Wild feet that go where none save Beauty's go! (II)

In an attempt to objectify love, as Millay did in "Into the golden vessel of great song," Ficke seeks to define love in highly sensuous terms:

> Beauty—what is it? A perfume without name:
> A sudden hush where clamor was before:
> Across the darkness a faint ghost of flame:
> A far sail, seen from a deserted shore. (III)

Ficke compares Millay to flames and the sun, revealing the height of their physical passion.

Although Ficke was hesitant to declare his love for Millay in his letters during this time, he boldly sings his love for her as physical and spiritual love begin to merge:

> In Beauty's name, I love you. Life's grim story
> Is swept with rainbow lights when you draw near.
> A singular and inescapable glory
> Comes from the sun when thoughts of you are here. (IV)

Ficke recognizes the brilliant, but fleeting, quality of their love as he compares their brief union to a rainbow, just as Millay did in "There is no shelter in you anywhere." Perhaps Ficke knew from the first that their love was too volatile to endure forever since he suggests that they must have "spaces in their togetherness":

> How savage is this destiny of ours
> That fashions music out of agony,
> And lets us hear, across the iron night,
> The wing-beats of each other's lonely flight! (IV)

After the initial excitement of purely sensual love, Ficke feels a more spiritual love for Millay, perhaps recalling the spiritual trust that grew in the first six years of their correspondence or their painful love letters exchanged after the three days in New York. Their love has taught him the timelessness and endurance of love, the nobility of life, the madness of love, the beauty of dreams instead of reality, the trust and holiness of love, and the spiritual union of two souls—sacred as the mystical union between God and man:

> As richer with all other loves you grow,
> The dearer is your wealth that I divine;
> All that enchants you is a golden glow—
> Ripening the grapes of our communion-wine. (X)

As Millay accepts the transcience of love in her early Village sonnets, Ficke dreads the demise of love through their
loss of affection or through physical death:

> Were we too dull, or too perversely clever?
> Was it conceit or wisdom sealed our eyes?
> What we have sought,—is it a quickening light,
> Or but the aurora of an Arctic night? (XII)

Rather than allowing their love to grow stale with time, Ficke
plans to end their love before they grow old:

> Thanks to our happy fate, we two shall meet
> Never more humanly than heretofore.
> No enmity of chance shall guide our feet
> Down paths of dreaming toward one twilight door. (XIII)

Doubting the endurance of love, he also questions the contra-
dictory nature of his beloved—"Actor, liar, prophetess, and
child"—qualities that both Dell and Wilson had observed earlier.

After the archetypal lover's doubt, Ficke ends *A Hymn to
Intellectual Beauty* with a deep reaffirmation of his faith in
their union. Time will exalt the two lovers, not for their pain
and sacrifice, but for their pride in love, as the glory of their
love will surpass even the senselessness of death—perhaps a
psychic foreshadowing of Millay reading poetry at Ficke's
funeral:

> But, if you should survive me, come, some day,
> To where, not knowing anything, I shall lie—
> And look down at the stupid mound of clay,
> And look up at the splendor of blue sky,—
> And know that neither you nor I could know
> All that our love meant to us long ago. (XVI)

With their love coming full cycle, Ficke feels their love will
endure through death and eternity:

> Everything left behind us like a dream
> Shall into an ambiguous darkness fade....
> You will be waiting, on that silent shore;
> And we shall speak. We never spoke before. (XVII)

From Thanksgiving Day, 1912, until his death on November 20, 1945, Arthur Davison Ficke played a significant role in the life and works of Edna St. Vincent Millay. In 1913 he was her "Spiritual Advisor," in 1920 "a part of Loveliness" to her, in 1945 her "sweet and trusted friend." Although their first meeting in 1918 touched them both with strong emotion, Millay did not suffer from unrequited love for the rest of her life. Yet at least three of Millay's sonnets and Ficke's sonnet sequence *A Hymn to Intellectual Beauty* crystallize their volatile, but wavering love, which they could not sustain until the "Twilight Door." Arthur Ficke was fortunate to find such a sympathetic and stable woman as Gladys Brown, just as Millay was perhaps blessed by her union with Eugen Boissevain, but the importance of the relationship between Ficke and Millay lies in the poetry their union inspired. Ficke himself partially explained the creative process involved in their reciprocal works:

> The aim of poetry is to capture those rare moments of the poet's experience when, for good or for evil, the consciousness of life sweeps through him like a flame....[23]

A charming, witty, and handsome man, Ficke easily became the symbol of idealized and selfless love for Millay. Although their love was not destined to endure, Millay learned from Ficke, as she also learned from Edmund Wilson, that love combines the physical, spiritual, and intellectual:

> Into the golden vessel of great song
> Let us pour all our passion: breast to breast
> Let other lovers lie, in love and rest:
> Not we,—articulate, so, but with the tongue
> Of all the world: the churning blood, the long
> Shuddering quiet, the desperate hot palms pressed
> Sharply together upon the escaping guest,
> The common soul, unguarded, and grown strong.

WITTER BYNNER

6

WHAT LIPS
MY LIPS HAVE KISSED:

Millay's Other Men

In all our lives, there are the private people, people who are not an integral part of our lives—the girl in the park who takes the stray kitten home, the seventy-year-old man who has traded his blue chip stock for a piece of canvas, the little girl who smiles up at you from her oversize package. With these people we touch and release, never to encounter again, and return to our everyday lives. Yet they do become a part of our lives, in a secret and private way. Millay too had her private people. Alexander MacKaig referred to her eighteen other love affairs, and Edmund Wilson suggested that her ex-admirers form an alumni association. Perhaps these other men in Millay's life should not be dismissed quite so lightly, for sometimes the minor threads in our lives intertwine to form the background on which the major figures stand out in sharp relief.

Through her intense relationships with Floyd Dell, Edmund Wilson, and Arthur Davison Ficke, Millay became the free and rebellious spirit of Greenwich Village. At the same time, however, there were other men who had a lesser impact on her life. Members of her coterie included Witter Bynner, the handsome poet; John Reed, radical political journalist; Allan Ross Macdougall, author, translator, and later editor of Millay's *Letters*: W. Adolphe Roberts, editor of *Ainslee's,* and Frank Crowninshield, editor of *Vanity Fair,* both of whom were instrumental in getting Millay's works published; and, Harrison Dowd, the sensual musician, novelist, and actor. The Millay alumni association includes many other names—Salomon de la Selva, Rollo Peters, Scudder Middleton, Pieter Miejer—but the entire roster could never be covered.

Witter Bynner

During her 1913 stay in New York, Millay enjoyed a round of parties and teas given in her honor by various New York literary celebrities because of the 1912 success of "Renascence." At a party given by Jessie Rittenhouse, she spotted a tall, athletic man with a Byronic face. When he came across the room to introduce himself, she laughed about his and Ficke's remark that "Renascence" had been written by a "brawny male of forty." After engaging in a frivolous conversation about smoking, Bynner and Millay sat on a small couch with a copy of "Renascence." Feeling too shy to read the poem aloud herself, Millay asked him to read it aloud, which he did in a deep, resonant voice.

Throughout her Village days, Bynner and Millay shared a deep appreciation and respect for each other's works. She greatly admired his one-act play about the white slave traffic, *Tiger.* Finding Bynner's poem "Union Square" in *Smart Set* a successful effort, Millay was extremely annoyed when he revised it; she wrote to Ficke, "He spoiled it when he changed it, and he ought to be ashamed."[1] Bynner thought "Renascence" was a phenomenal poem but did not hesitate to refer to "Interim" and "The Suicide" as "long, rather callow poems." In an article in the *New Republic* in 1924, Bynner pointed out some minor flaws in Millay's work but boldly asserted that "The Waste Land" grew "stale and unprofitable" alongside "Renascence."[2] At the same time, neither felt awkward extolling his *own* merit, as is exemplified by Millay's candid remark to Bynner in 1920, "I am becoming very famous."[3] Until her death, Bynner served as a source of emotional and artistic support for Millay, even when her work had reached a low ebb. Knowing very well that *Make Bright the Arrows* was an inferior book of verse, she felt free to write to Bynner, "Some of the reviews were insolent to the point of being really 'actionable,' I think. Not that any of this mattered at all."[4] Yet Millay did suffer because of her diminishing reputation, and she no doubt drew strength from the artistic integrity Bynner perceived in her.

As important as their intellectual relationship, however, was the deep emotional bond between Bynner and Millay. The humor and honesty Millay shared with Bynner emerge in a letter she dashed off to him in 1920. Irritated that he and Ficke had stayed in the Orient so long, Millay writes, "When are you two boys coming home?...I miss you like hell." Even though she comments on her success, she frankly admits her difficulties with her publisher, Mitchell Kennerly, who misrepresented her contract to her and refused to answer her calls and letters. And even Millay, liberated before her time, is not ashamed to admit to being vulnerable when she says she wishes Bynner and Ficke would come home and beat up the errant publisher![5]

Most puzzling in the Millay/Bynner affair were their abortive marriage plans. In late 1921, Millay received a letter from Ficke concerning Bynner's letter to her proposing marriage, which she had never received. Nevertheless, she agreed to marry him, even though she expressed some doubts: "Do you really want me to marry you?—Because if you really want me to, I will."[6] A month later, Millay was having second thoughts, fearing the hazards of an "earthly marriage" and viewing marriage per se as "a series of disagreements, misunderstandings, adjustments, ill-adjustments, and readjust-ments."[7] The question of marrying Bynner also was confused by her continued and freely admitted love for Ficke, al-though she avowed that people can always love more than one person. The matter was finally resolved when Ficke inter-vened by writing a letter discouraging the union and sending exact copies to both Millay and Bynner. One year after Bynner's original proposal, Millay airily wrote Ficke, "As for Hal [Bynner], there's not the slightest danger that I shall marry him: he has jilted me!"[8]

While the facts of this situation seem farcical, the implica-tions are more serious and reveal aspects of each personality. Even though Edna was fond of Hal, this love was not the all-consuming romance she had with Ficke. For all her outward independence, perhaps Millay was beginning to feel lonely and rejected because of two impending marriages—Arthur Ficke to Gladys Brown and Norma Millay to Charles Ellis. With a facade of bravado, she wrote Norma, "Anybody can get married. It happens all the time."[9] On Bynner's part, he too may have been taking the cue from his best friend Arthur, who planned to marry Gladys, as well as hoping to assuage Edna's feeling of isolation. He also might have been seeking a plausible mask for, or a diversion from, his homo-sexuality. Gladys Brown Ficke pointed out that Bynner loved Vincent Millay mildly but loved Robert Hunt dearly.[10] Despite their reasons for marriage, they probably rejected it because of Bynner's homosexuality.

As Village compatriots, Witter Bynner and Edna Millay shared a deep respect for each other's work. As devoted friends, they also made pretenses of marriage. After they left the Village, they retained an open relationship, tempered with humor. When Millay asked Bynner to visit her at Stee-pletop in 1935, she queried, "Can you come to Steepletop sometime in May. Can you do it without bringing your mother? I know she's grand and all that...but I'm going to die in a few days, and I have no time left except for people I'm crazy about."[11]

John Reed

Romantic, adventurous, with dark flashing eyes, John Reed was considered one of the most radical political figures of Greenwich Village. He had been stirred to social activism while reporting the Paterson silk workers' strike and the Ludlow miners' strike in 1913.[12] When Floyd Dell introduced Reed to Millay in 1918, he was facing charges of treason in the first *Masses'* trial along with Floyd Dell, Art Young, and John Sloan. By this time, his involvement with the Russian Revolution had become so intense that he returned from Russia barely in time for the second *Masses'* trial.[13]

In the Village, Millay was not especially political, but Reed may well have nurtured the seeds of social activism that later matured into her defense of Sacco and Vanzetti, her involvement with women's rights, and her support of America's involvement in World War II. Possibly she read his book about the Russian Revolution, *Ten Days that Shook the World*, and absorbed his adventures while reporting strikes, revolutions, and instances of social injustice. By 1918 Millay's social consciousness certainly had begun to germinate when she explained the idea of *Aria da Capo*, her bitter antiwar play, to Reed, asking for his suggestions and hoping for his approval.[14]

A year after the second *Masses'* trial, Reed returned to Russia, fought with the Communists, and died there of typhoid fever. Hearing of his death, Milly was so moved that she wrote the sonnet "Lord Archer, Death" and possibly another poem, "To One Who Might Have Borne a Message,"[15] to the dark-haired journalist.

The tone of "Lord Archer, Death," is similar to Millay's bitter resentment of death in "Dirge Without Music":

Lord Archer, Death, whom sent you in your stead?
What faltering prentice fumbled at your bow,
That now should wander with the insanguine dead
In whom forever the bright blood must flow?
Or is it rather that impairing Time
Renders yourself so random, or so dim?
Or are you sick of shadows and would climb
A while to light, a while detaining him?
For know, this was no mortal youth, to be
Of you confounded, but a heavenly guest,
Assuming earthly garb for love of me,
And hell's demure attire for love of jest:
Bringing me asphodel and a dark feather,
He will return, and we shall laugh together!

The meaning of the octave is obvious—Death did not care enough to come himself; he sent an apprentice. Then in the sestet Millay is even clearer: she will not accept death; perhaps Reed will even return from the dead, and they will laugh at the whole idea, for Reed is a "heavenly guest"—above death.

Enshrined as a martyr to the Russian Revolution, Reed served as a symbol of political radicalism and social upheaval. Possibly Reed encouraged Millay to develop the social consciousness manifested several years after her Village days.

Allan Ross Macdougall

Warm, generous, and gentle, Allan Ross Macdougall was one of the most active literary figures in the Village during Millay's era. His involvement with various newspapers later led to his becoming international editor for the Chicago *Tribune* in 1921. At the same time, he was writing a moving biography of Isadora Duncan, the beautiful dancer, *The Gourmet's Almanac*, and translating the Belgian classic *Tyl Ulenspiegel* into English. Long after his Village days, he carefully collected and edited Millay's *Letters* and interviewed Eugen Boissevain with warmth and candor about his marriage to the famous poet, which resulted in the important article "Husband of A Genius" in *The Delineator.*

Sharing criticism and appreciation of his works with Macdougall, Millay's relationship with Macdougall was marked by
fondness and innocence. Occasionally, Millay and Macdougall
degenerated into insane silliness when they shared one of
their favorite passions—Krazy Kat cartoons and poems. When
Macdougall was leaving for Paris in 1921, Millay whimsically
jotted down this pleasant doggerel:

> Blessing on the Head of A. R. M.
> (On the occasion of his going abroad a-minstrelling)
>
> Allin dear, li'l' wisdim toot',
> Spirit uv eternil yout',
> Bless you up and bless you down,
> Bless you into London town;
> Bless you round and round about,
> Bless you into France and out;
> Let your sayin' an' your singin'
> Set the bells o' London ringin'
> Let your singin' an' your sayin'
> Set the beads o' Paris prayin';
> Let the sun and rain so sweet
> Bless the road before your feet,
> Bless the ditch you lay your head in,
> Bless the weeds will be your beddin';
> Allin dear, li'l' wisdim toot'
> Edna luvs you,—thet's the trut'.[16]

A close textual analysis of this poem would be ludicrous; suf-
fice it to say that Millay was fond of Macdougall.

In addition to their mutual mania about Krazy Kat car-
toons, Millay and Macdougall admired each other's work.
When he sent her the proofs for his biography of Isadora
Duncan, she checked the pages with her usual thoroughness
and noted this minor point: "...Instead of saying 'Tunis,
North Africa,' just say 'Tunis....' There's something so uncos-
mopolitan, so provincial in the sound of the added 'North
Africa....' "[17] Not only did Macdougall admire Millay's

poetry, he also made an effort to have it published. In 1920, he arranged for one of her poems to be published in *The Nation*, and when he left for Europe he carried copies of Millay's poetry and *Aria da Capo* to British publishers.

On a more personal level, Millay did not feel a need to burden Macdougall with pretensions. With feeling, she wrote him of music, "Indeed, with music, I should wish to die....All that remains is Bach, I find that I never lose Bach."[18] When Millay left for Europe, Macdougall was thoughtful enough to send her roses, and when he lacked money she tactfully sent him a check.

Despite their close relationship, intimacy between Millay and Macdougall was checked by his homosexuality, according to an anonymous source. Regardless, Millay is indebted to Macdougall, not only for his thoughtfulness, but also for placing her works and, much later, for editing her letters.

W. Adolphe Roberts

Returning from Europe as a war correspondent in 1918, W. Adolphe Roberts became editor of *Ainslee's*, the magazine that Edmund Wilson considered "trashy." Honest and humorous, Roberts himself recognized *Ainslee's* lack of great literary merit. In his unpublished memoir of Edna Millay, "Tiger Lily," the young editor explains the attitude of the philistine publishers: "Their conception of publishing was to buy paper in the cheapest market, to hire an eccentric to do something or other to the paper, and then to sell it for a little more than they had paid for it."[19] Undaunted by this climate, Roberts decided that he would publish the finest poetry in the United States even though he could only pay fifty cents a line. When Salomon de la Selva, the young Nicaraguan poet, told Roberts he thought Stephen Vincent Benét and Edna St. Vincent Millay the best of the younger poets, Roberts dropped Millay a note asking her to bring some of her poems to *Ainslee's* office, which she did on a September morning in 1918. Although they talked of poetry, Roberts was most struck by the beauty and charm of Millay, who immediately reminded him of a tiger lily.

From this brief meeting in 1918 sprang a three-year friend-ship between Millay and Roberts. A week or so after they met they began frequenting Mouquin's on Sixth Avenue, the Lafayette on University Place, and several unpretentious, bohemian French restaurants downtown. Like most of their friends, they scoffed at Prohibition and drank excellent wines. Once they went to a large party, the Kit Kat ball of the club of illustrators, but generally they preferred intimate dinners, when they discussed love, poetry, and the theater.[20]

As their relationship developed, Millay began to replay the old pattern of many of her Village affairs. Her charm, wit, and beauty caused Roberts to become so deeply involved that he later wrote, "...more deeply than she guessed or prob-ably cared I wanted it to be an exchange between us only." But Millay, free spirit of the Village, would not be placed in a cage. To avoid commitment, she told Roberts that the only man she had ever loved was married and would probably never love her. This man, of course, was Arthur Davison Ficke. To make her point even clearer, Millay taunted Roberts by frequently announcing when she left him that she was going to visit Pieter Miejer, a virile, handsome Javanese printmaker. Unlike some of Millay's more insecure lovers, Roberts kept his jealousy in check and concluded, "I...took her temperament exactly as I found it and preached no ser-mons."

Most important in the Roberts/Millay affair, however, was the vital role he played in getting her work published. During their first visit, Roberts accepted Millay's poem "Daphne" for the next issue of *Ainslee's*, then published all except two of her poems in 1919, as well as most of her work in 1920-21. Although Roberts recognized the genius of Millay's poetry, he still could pay her only the modest sum the publishers allowed. In January 1919, however, Millay and Roberts came up with a more lucrative plan for the financially strained poet. She would write fiction, which they concurred was "potboiling," under the pseudonym Nancy Boyd. Not only did Millay write seven Nancy Boyd stories during 1919-20, somewhat contrived tales of young women possessed of varying degrees of feminism, she also wrote a novelette, *The Seventh Stair,* for which Roberts was able to pay $400. By 1921, Millay had received enough acclaim to attract the attention of *Vanity Fair*, a better-paying and more prestigious magazine than *Ainslee's*. When Millay left *Ainslee's*, Roberts with characteristic honesty and generosity wrote, "By 1921 her name had disappeared from *Ainslee's*, rightly and inevitably. *Vanity Fair* had the privilege of launching her as a success with a public that counted."[21]

Although Edna Millay did not fall deeply in love with W. Adolphe Roberts, she enjoyed their lively discussions and quiet dinners and appreciated his many small favors, such as his loaning her his apartment while he was away so that she would have a quiet place to write. Modest as he was about his role in Millay's career, Roberts deserves great credit for publishing and promoting, against substantial obstacles at *Ainslee's*, the work of the poet he considered "the greatest woman poet since Sappho."

Frank Crowninshield

Clever and urbane, Frank Crowninshield had inherited a fine appreciation of literature and art and confidence in his critical abilities from his distinguished Boston family. Under his editorship, *Vanity Fair* featured many of the most outstanding writers of the day and catered to a rather sophisticated audience. After Millay's success with *Ainslee's* and with encouragement from Edmund Wilson, Crowninshield began publishing some of Millay's work in 1920 and by 1921 persuaded her to make a total transition to *Vanity Fair.*

Throughout his relationship with Millay, Crowninshield maintained a paternal, protective attitude toward the young poet. Shortly after Millay's move to *Vanity Fair*, Crowninshield teasingly complained of the difficulty of having two of his assistant editors, Edmund Wilson and John Peale Bishop, in love with one of his most brilliant contributors.[22] Even after her Village days, Millay retained a warm affection for "Crownie." On March 17, 1926, she wrote him, "You will never know how your sweet funny little letters cheer me up. What a nice person you are."[23] In 1947 Crowninshield visited Steepletop only to discover that Millay was not there. In a letter of apology, Millay wrote, "Anyway, I still love you, even if you do hate me, and I wish you A Happy New Year."[24]

By featuring Millay's poetry in *Vanity Fair*, Crowninshield was responsible for a tremendous surge in Millay's popularity. Again with Wilson's encouragement, Crowninshield also turned one of Millay's dreams—a trip to Europe—into reality. Perhaps he realized that Millay needed a change of pace, since she had just suffered a minor nervous breakdown and felt that her poetry was becoming sterile. Crowninshield appointed Millay foreign correspondent to Europe, where she would write two articles per month—one under her name, the other under Nancy Boyd—for her regular monthly salary.[25]

In comparison with W. Adolphe Roberts, Crowninshield seems the lesser influence on Millay's work. Certainly Crowninshield did not take the intensely personal interest in Millay that Roberts did, nor was he forced to work under the financial handicap that Roberts was.[26] Edmund Wilson accused Crowninshield of being shallow and unreliable. Although Wilson tended to be unduly harsh in many of his judgments, in one case perhaps he was justified. At times Crowninshield urged Millay to sign her own name to her Nancy Boyd pieces, since the Millay signature would automatically double the price of the article. Millay strenuously objected since the pen name served to differentiate her popular prose from her poetry, a dichotomy Roberts clearly understood.

The most important contributions that Frank Crowninshield made to Edna Millay's career were featuring her works in *Vanity Fair* and arranging her trip to Europe. As a paternal figure, he cherished a warm affection and respect for Millay. Although she lived in constant fear that Crownie would chastise her for missing deadlines on her stories, he never criticized her. After wishing Crownie a Happy New Year in 1947, Millay wrote, "And I wish myself a happy new year, too,—a year in which I shall see you and talk with you."[27]

Harrison Dowd

Shortly after her arrival in the Village, Millay met Harrison Dowd, a sensual, but shy, musician, novelist, and actor. A close friend of Allan Ross Macdougall, Dowd was the modest, Renaissance man whom everyone liked. Late in 1917, Millay arrived home one night to find Harrison Dowd waiting for her. After much urging, Dowd began playing the piano for her, and she was amazed to learn that he knew entire opera scores by heart and had even set part of "A Shropshire Lad" by A. E. Housman (one of Millay's favorite poets) to music. After performing a virtual concert, he turned to Millay and asked, "How does it feel to be a success?"[28]

For many reasons, Dowd would have been an ideal suitor for Millay. Since at one time in her life Millay trained to become a concert pianist, she certainly shared Dowd's love of music. (A few years later, she was appalled because Roberts did not have a deep appreciation of music.) With catholic taste and abilities in music, Dowd hired a hall and sang popular songs to the "idle rich," played the piano in a jazz orchestra in Berlin, and created a poetic adaptation of Mozart's *La Finta Giardiniera*, which was produced by the Intimate Opera Company at the Mayfair Theatre in New York in 1927.[29]

When Millay's antiwar play *Aria da Capo* opened in 1919,

Harrison Dowd portrayed the male lead, Pierrot. Not only a musician and actor, Dowd also wrote a novel, *The Night Air,* which Millay praised, appropriately enough, in musical terms.

> I wish I had the time to write you all the things I want to say about your fine book....Only a very musical person could have written it. Not that there is anything at all obviously *musical* about it! I refer to changes of key, changes in tempo, that sort of thing, beautifully done. I get so awfully tired of books that sit down to the typewriter in the key of C Major and in 4/4 time and plod right along like that to the end.[30]

While many of Millay's lovers and thinkers in the Village had rather fragile egos, Dowd was very secure in his own intellect and abilities. More gentle than many men, he was not afraid to acknowledge Millay's success. Why then did he and Millay not establish a long-term relationship? One reputable source who insists on remaining anonymous cites Dowd's homosexuality as the reason.

Therefore, in the roster of Millay's private people, three of the six men were homosexual—Witter Bynner, Allan Ross Macdougall, and Harrison Dowd. All were bright, versatile, intelligent—qualities that Millay respected. Her attraction to these men could be explained partially by her transient lesbian period, but that argument is a little suspect. What attracted Millay to these men was probably their quality of gentleness, which allowed her to admit fear, vulnerability, humanity. Millay's husband, Eugen Boissevain, though decidedly not homosexual, combined these qualities of gentleness and humility with physical prowess and emotional strength.

As for Millay's other three private people, Crowninshield stands apart, for he had only a fatherly interest in Millay, combined with his interest in getting her works published. For all his success in publishing her works, Millay well may have rejected Roberts because of his ineptitude at music. Finally, Millay's creative fancy was trapped by the premature death of John Reed, who may have imbued her with the idea

of social consciousness. Nevertheless, all six men were important, and any could have served as the model for the following sonnet:

> What lips my lips have kissed, and where, and why,
> I have forgotten, and what arms have lain
> Under my head till morning; but the rain
> Is full of ghosts tonight, that tap and sigh
> Upon the glass and listen for reply,
> And in my heart there stirs a quiet pain
> For unremembered lads that not again
> Will turn to me at midnight with a cry.
> Thus in the winter stands the lonely tree,
> Nor knows what birds have vanished one by one,
> Yet knows its boughs more silent than before:
> I cannot say what loves have come and gone,
> I only know that summer sang in me
> A little while, that in me sings no more.

7

LOVE IS NOT ALL:

Eugen Boissevain

A soft breeze from the Hudson River bathed the small group of artists and liberals who chatted quietly beneath Rousseau green trees. Lightly clasping hands, the tall, athletic man and the small, slender woman seemed oblivious to their friends. After her five-year spree in the Village, Edna Millay had found love and comfort in a most unlikely man—Eugen Boissevain, a Dutch coffee importer twelve years her senior who understood swimming and rowing better than poetry, yet cherished his elfin "Aidna" for her independence and talent. As the ceremony drew near, Edna decided she wanted to look like a bride, despite her earlier derision of marriage. Catching the spontaneity of the moment, Norma Millay Ellis whipped a long veil out of mosquito netting, plucked a cluster of white roses from a nearby bush, and placed the wreath and veil on her sister's long, auburn hair. Away from the clutter and noisy humanity of Greenwich Village, the intimate group—Arthur Ficke, Gladys Brown, Norma and Charles Ellis, and a few other close friends and family members—encircled the couple in the simple beauty of the landscape. After less than three months of intense emotional and sexual rapport and little preparation for a wedding, Eugen, realizing that he did not have a ring for Edna, borrowed one from his maid Hattie. As sunlight seeped through the dense leaves of the Croton lawn, Edna Millay married Eugen Boissevain on July 18, 1923.[1]

Born in Amsterdam, Holland, in 1880 to an affluent, educated, and influential family, Eugen Boissevain received a solid education from tutors and private schools, but his forte lay more in sports than in fine arts. A skilled athlete, he rowed in the Henley Regatta on the Thames in England and was asked to enter the Diamond Sculls, the most competitive of rowing contests. He maintained a trim figure throughout his life and sustained his interest in sports by swimming and playing tennis with Edna after their marriage. Unlike Millay's unconventional family, Eugen's maternal grandfather had been Provost of Trinity College in Dublin, and his father was the publisher of *Algemeen Handelsbled*, Holland's leading newspaper. As a token of respect for the Boissevain family, President Theodore Roosevelt received Eugen at the White House when he visited the United States as a youth.[2]

Although Eugen was a connoisseur of the arts, his primary talent lay in business. For many years, he owned a coffee, sugar, and copra import firm in downtown Manhattan, but when coffee imports from Java were suspended during World War I Boissevain suffered grave business losses. Far from being a millionaire, by the time he married Millay in 1923, Boissevain's fortune was reduced to only two or three thousand dollars.[3]

Although he was not as artistic as Millay's other Village suitors, Eugen Boissevain was a gentle, stable man, possessing one particular quality that strongly attracted Millay—a profound respect for intelligent women. In 1913 in London, Eugen had married his first wife, Inez Milholland, a Vassar graduate, astute lawyer, and champion of women's rights. Always supporting her beliefs and activities, he often accompanied her to her many lectures and endorsed her involvement in New York shirtwaist and laundry strikes. In 1915 he stood by quietly and proudly while his statuesque, blond wife rode a white horse down Fifth Avenue leading the Suffrage Parade. Later that year, Eugen escorted Inez to Vassar, where she became the "idol of the undergraduates," including Edna St. Vincent Millay.[4]

Secure in his own ego, Eugen resisted meddling in Inez's career while still serving as a supportive influence. His psychoanalysis by Jung in Zurich left Boissevain free of any traces of "male superiority" and prone to "the art of casually blurting out...the intimate truth."[5] Agreeing to a free love type of marriage with Inez, which released both parties from conventional restrictions, Eugen felt emotional trust more important than purely physical fidelity. In 1916 Inez collapsed halfway through a lecture, and Eugen carried her back to their hotel, where she died shortly afterwards of pernicious anemia. On her deathbed Inez crystallized their deep spiritual bond as she whispered to Eugen, "...go out and lead another life."[6] After his three-year marriage to the beautiful suffragette, Eugen was well suited for his second life with another talented and independent woman—Edna St. Vincent Millay.

Shocked and exhausted by the great void left by Inez's sudden death, Eugen gradually began to piece together the fabric of his second life. After several months he moved into Max Eastman's New York apartment, where he first met Edna Millay. In 1917 Floyd Dell took Edna and Norma Millay to meet Eugen Boissevain at Eastman's apartment, but Dell found the visit a dismal failure: "It was for some reason a stiff, dull evening; everybody was bored. I was annoyed with the girls and disgusted with our boorish hosts."[7] Throughout the evening, Millay remained withdrawn, drab, and bored, sparking with interest only when Eugen spoke of Inez Milholland, Millay's college idol. Another meeting a few weeks later left Edna and Eugen equally unimpressed with

each other. During the next six years, while Millay enjoyed
her many lovers and thinkers in the Village, Eastman and
Boissevain moved their bachelor quarters to Croton-on-Hudson, a picturesque town an hour from New York by train,
which became a mecca for communists in the 1930's.

In the late spring of 1923, Edna Millay, Arthur Davison
Ficke, Gladys Brown, Floyd Dell, Max Eastman, and Eugen
Boissevain met at the Dorris Stevens/Dudley Malone Mt. Airy
home in Croton for a party, where they spontaneously
decided to enact "a delicious farcical invention, at once
Rabelaisian and romantic." When Eugen and Edna were
paired off as the lovers in the farce, Dell had "the unusual
privilege of seeing a man and a girl fall in love with each other
violently and in public...."[8] Less than three months after
their third meeting, Eugen and Edna were married in front of
the Eastman/Boissevain house, across the road from the
home where they fell in love. During this time, they enjoyed
the intense relationship that continued until Eugen's death
over twenty years later.

The popular fancy was intrigued by Millay's marriage. The
Chicago *Times* ran a five-column article entitled "Has Happiness Come to Repay / Fair Edna St. Vincent Millay" and sub-
titled "She Married as She lived—On a Moment's Impulse."
The *Times* exclaimed, "She, to whom freedom is a religion,
submitted to the matrimonial yoke...." Millay was a "feminine Percy Bysshe Shelley," "a gay, free spirit of romance
and joy." The *Times* mused, "Greenwich Village had pre-
dicted that she would never marry, that she was too fond of
her freedom...that Edna would choose single blessedness in
preference to the slavery of marriage."[9]

Immediately after their intimate wedding in Croton, Eugen
drove his bride to New York for a serious intestinal operation, foreshadowing the fatherly role he played throughout
their marriage. After Millay left the hospital, the Boissevains
spent a few months at Eugen's Croton home, moved into the

Holley Hotel off Washington Square in the fall, and in January 1924 found a charming house around the corner from the Cherry Lane Theatre and a few blocks from Chumley's. This "dollhouse" at 75½ Bedford Street was three stories high, thirty feet tall, nine and a half feet wide, had a fireplace in each room, and an artistic, miniature courtyard behind the house. Almost immediately, Millay left for a two-month reading tour, which would enable her to repay some of her mother's debts and her own. During her trip, she wrote Eugen of the poor room service at the Windermere Hotel in Chicago, which was "the God-damndest place I ever set an unwary foot in." The trains were uncomfortable, but she could have endured the experience had Eugen been with her. "How entirely, *totally, ABSOLUTELY* different everything would be if you were in this chair beside me." Exhausted, Millay returned to New York, and in March she and Eugen left for a six-month trip around the world, which they were able to make with some of the money Millay had made on the reading tour and a few thousand dollars remaining from Eugen's business. But they were forced to travel second class, and in Japan they usually walked instead of hiring transportation.[10]

Returning from their world tour to their Bedford Street house, Edna and Eugen decided that city life was too hectic for them. Two years earlier Millay had written in *Exiled,* "I am weary of words and people, / Sick of the city, wanting the sea." Although the Boissevains did not find their beach home until later, they discovered a run-down farmhouse in Austerlitz, New York, which they immediately decided to buy and named Steepletop after a white wildflower that flourished on the seven hundred acres of land.[11] A tunnel of trees enclosed the unpaved road leading to the large, white clapboard house with its beautifully landscaped lawn. By the summer of 1925, Eugen and Edna moved into Steepletop, even though the repairs were not quite completed. In a letter to her mother, Millay described renovating Steepletop with her usual disdain for the mundane. The plumbing was all connected, but there was no water, so they all bathed in the brook. Six masons, four plumbers, two servants, and fifteen berry-picking children were living at Steepletop, although the Boissevains had moved to Austerlitz for privacy. Their servant Julia lost her mind and thought that Eugen and Edna planned to hang her from a rafter, and Joseph, Millay reported, "pissed in the berries, so we don't employ him any more." Yet Millay gradually lost her intoxication with life as she settled into the soundless pace of Steepletop. Her Greenwich Village days were over.

After Millay abandoned the Village and her single life, her poetry lost much of its spontaneous personal quality and gained a meditative, omniscient caste. Many people believed that Eugen Boissevain contributed little to this transition in his second wife's work. Norma Millay Ellis says that Eugen had no effect whatsoever on Millay's work,[12] just as Gladys Brown Ficke thinks Eugen's influence on Millay was insignificant,[13] but Deems Taylor feels, "Her husband, Eugen Jan Boissevain...profoundly influenced her work."[14] Particularly in her later works, Eugen Boissevain seems to have had a noticeable effect on the poetry of Edna St. Vincent Millay.

Although Boissevain had only a general knowledge of literature, he cherished a great respect for his wife's work. He told Allan Ross Macdougall, "If she wrote *one* sonnet a year it seems to me important that she be free to write that sonnet." Boissevain found Millay's mind to be "acutely intelligent and powerful. All the things are in her which makes one at peace again with the human race...." After his marriage to Millay, he felt that "Any day I may have an hour of extraordinary beauty in my life." He cheerfully sublimated his work and desires to those of his wife: "It is so obvious to anyone that Vincent is more important than I am. Anyone can buy and sell coffee....But anyone cannot write poetry."[15]

Boissevain did not influence the form and syntax of Millay's poetry, but he well may have contributed to her growing social consciousness, a theme of her later works. He had encouraged Inez Milholland's battle for women's rights and had shared living quarters for five years with Max Eastman, who advocated peace, socialism, revolution, birth control, and reform in correctional institutions, first as editor of the *Masses* and later as editor of the *Liberator*. As early as November 1923, Millay wrote the sonnet, "The Pioneer," which deals with women's rights, later including the inscription "To Inez Milholland" as a tribute to both Eugen and his first wife. In 1927, Millay's involvement in the Sacco-Vanzetti case inspired her to write "Justice Denied in Massachusetts." When Millay went to Boston to picket for the cause, Eugen accompanied her and put up twenty-five dollars for bail after she was arrested.

In his personal relationship with Millay, Boissevain seemed to serve as a father figure. Not only did he draw her bath and rub her back,[16] he also assumed most of the household tasks, because he felt that Millay should not be bothered by housework, which she hated, and because they had difficulty keeping servants at Steepletop. Boissevain cooked, washed, directed the household and estate, dictated letters, managed the business affairs, charmingly dismissed unwelcome guests,[17] and finally was forced to post a sign: "Visitors received only by appointment."[18]

In many ways, Boissevain's protective attitude eased the physical and mental burdens that increasingly plagued Millay after her marriage. This extremely kind and strong man urged Millay to seek the medical aid she so needed. On June 8, 1923, she wrote her mother that she was being X-rayed and examined thoroughly by several diagnosticians. She added, "Eugen has been taking me to these doctors; probably by myself I would never have done it." Eugen also served as an attentive nurse through Millay's various illnesses, especially

during the last ten years of her life. Burning her candle at
both ends in her Village days had left Millay drained both
physically and emotionally. Suffering from migraine headaches,[19] and alcoholism[20] in her later days at Steepletop,
Millay often would inject morphine before guests arrived to
give herself the necessary "high" to be a charming hostess.[21]
In an unpublished portion of a letter to Witter Bynner, Millay
confessed, "I am at present under the influence of hashish,
gin, bad poetry, love, morphine and hunger,—otherwise I
could not be writing you even this."[22] Several years later,
Millay reportedly overcame her drug problem. Eugen had a
calming effect on Millay's complex and sometimes neurotic
personality, as Edmund Wilson noted during his 1929 visit to
Steepletop:

> I had a curious and touching impression, as Edna sat quiet in a big
> chair, that—torn and distracted by winds that had swept her
> through many seas—she had been towed into harbor and moored,
> that she was floating at anchor there.[23]

Eugen even intervened in Millay's minor domestic problems.
After arbitrating many quarrels between Norma and Edna
Millay, Eugen finally refused to let Norma visit her sister.[24]

At first glance, Eugen Boissevain would seem to have been
the perfect husband for Millay. Sharing the same sort of free
love relationship with Millay as he had with Milholland,
Eugen told Allan Ross Macdougall, "Unless you are a fool
and so conceited as to think you are the greatest, the most
wonderful man in the world, how can you expect a woman
to love only you!" Edmund Wilson noted, "Yet she continued from time to time, to follow her old pattern of escape by
breaking away from her domestic arrangements."[25] One
leading American scholar who prefers to remain anonymous
recalls a Russian who accompanied Millay to one of her
reading engagements. After the event was over, he gallantly
began jumping over fence after fence in the dark to find some
gin for Millay. Despite her extramarital affairs Millay

remained emotionally faithful to Eugen. Finding ordinary norms of marriage ridiculous, Edna often laughed with Eugen as he jovially told of his exploits with a servant girl from a neighboring farm.[26]

Always swimming in the nude, Edna and Eugen encouraged their guests to disrobe and join them in their small pool at Steepletop. As mentioned earlier, while the Boissevains were visiting the Fickes in New Mexico in 1926, Ficke took a number of highly artistic dance poses of Edna and Gladys in the nude, and later the two couples posed nude, sitting around a table sipping drinks. Free of the conventional restrictions of marriage, Millay was able to retain some of the freedom she had enjoyed in the Village.

A handsome and charming man, Boissevain did not resent his wife's popularity and prominence; when referred to as "Mr. Edna St. Vincent Millay," he would slap his thigh with glee and roar with laughter. Secure in his own abilities, he had a "complete lack of egotism" when others compared him with Millay.[27] He was an excellent conversationalist, very young in spirit, masculine, and lovable.[28] Although he adored Millay in much the same way Floyd Dell did, he was not a placid individual but rather "a very temperamental man who only quarreled with his best friends."[29]

At times Boissevain's patronizing attitude toward Millay tended to curb her free spirit. In 1940 Millay was asked to read a poem at the United China Relief Banquet. Nervous and physically sick, Millay said, "I can't sit with strangers only....Please, I must have Eugen sitting beside me. Believe me, it's true. I don't know what will happen if he isn't here. Please, please—otherwise, I'll have to go home!"[30] When Edmund Wilson visited Steepletop in 1948, Eugen greeted him with, "I'll go and get my child," causing Wilson to remark, "At moments he would baby her in a way...that had evidently become habitual...."[31] Although Eugen was a great source of strength to Millay, he perhaps did her a disservice by allowing her to become so dependent on him.

On a personal level, Millay's marriage to Boissevain was relatively successful. He respected her work to the point of insisting on giving up his own importing business. He adored Millay's independence and intelligence, just as he had respected those qualities in his first wife. He was not horrified by the thought of extramarital affairs, and he provided Millay with emotional and some financial security; he was "lover and husband and the best friend she ever had."[32]

Despite the personal comfort and peace Eugen Boissevain gave Edna St. Vincent Millay, he perhaps was not the perfect husband for her. In fact, marriage per se well might have contributed to the declining quality of her poetry. Creativity, by its very nature, does not involve a state of contentment, but rather a state of indecision, of seeking new problems, new answers, new definitions, new expressions of old ideas. Creativity frequently decrees that the man or woman be at odds with society, which rests in a comfortable balance, the status quo. Therefore, the artist, in order to become the innovator, the original thinker, must seem to his peers an eccentric.[33] Removed from the swirling humanity of the Village, the uncertainty of single life, to the tranquility of Steepletop and the security of Boissevain's love, Millay well may have lost much of the creative tension so necessary to the serious artist. If Millay had not had Eugen to scare the wolves from her door, perhaps she would have hurled stones at the beasts herself.

From a professional standpoint then, Millay may not have chosen the perfect husband. After she left Greenwich Village, she produced two volumes of poetry—*The Harp-Weaver and Other Poems* (1923) and *The Buck in the Snow and Other Poems* (1928)—that retain much of the spontaneity of her Village poems. *The Harp-Weaver* contains such fine sonnets as "Love is not blind. I see with single eye," "I know I am but summer to your heart," "I pray you if you love me, bear my joy," "Pity me not because the light of day," "What lips my lips have kissed," and "Euclid alone has looked on Beauty bare." *The Buck in the Snow* contains one of Millay's master-pieces, "Dirge Without Music," as well as "Moriturus" and "On Hearing a Symphony of Beethoven." Certainly the first lines of "I know I am but summer to your heart" capture Millay's basic skepticism and intellectual probing of love:

> I know I am but summer to your heart,
> And not the full four seasons of the year;
> And you must welcome from another part
> Such noble moods as are not mine, my dear.
> No gracious weight of golden fruits to sell
> Have I, nor any wise and wintry thing;
> And I have loved you all too long and well
> To carry still the high sweet breast of Spring.

But Millay's social consciousness crept into *The Buck in the Snow* with "Justice Denied in Massachusetts," "The Anguish," "Hangman's Oak," and "The Pioneer." *Fatal Interview* (1931), a sequence of fifty-two love sonnets, definitely serves as a transition from Millay's spontaneous Village poetry to work of a more philosophical cast. Harriet Monroe comments, "In *Fatal Interview*...her powers...accept lower grounds for its exercise," and Allen Tate feels the volume lacked "distinction of emotional quality."

On November 17, 1923, four months after her wedding, Millay went to Washington "with a whole bunch of suffra-gettes" for ceremonies organized by the National Women's Party to commemorate the seventy-fifth anniversary of the Equal Rights Meeting of 1848. The next day in the crypt of the Capitol, a statue was unveiled in memory of Lucretia Mott, Susan B. Anthony, and Elizabeth Cady Stanton. For the occasion, Millay read her recently composed sonnet "The Pioneer," which insists on women's rights, especially in the last lines:

The stone will perish; I shall be twice dust.
Only my standard on a taken hill
Can cheat the mildew and the red-brown rust
And make immortal my adventurous will.
Even now the silk is tugging at the staff:
Take up the song; forget the epitaph.

By 1927 Millay's social consciousness had broadened to a concern over the Sacco-Vanzetti case, which aroused the indignation of many liberals. On April 15, 1920, Nicola Sacco and Bartolomeo Vanzetti, two nearly illiterate Italians, were arrested; on September 11, they were tried and found guilty of murder. Sacco and Vanzetti served as ideal suspects because they were anarchists, pacifists, and foreigners, and their broken English led to further confusion and implication during their questioning. For the next seven years, a complex chain of legal maneuvering was all that stood between these men and the electric chair.

From 1920 to 1927, many lawyers and writers, including Upton Sinclair and John Dos Passos, worked to free Sacco and Vanzetti, but their efforts were partially thwarted by the postwar hysteria against radicals and the prejudice of Judge Webster Thayer of Massachusetts. By 1927, the Sacco-Vanzetti case had attracted international attention: George Bernard Shaw and Albert Einstein wrote in behalf of the two men; riots erupted in Buenos Aires, Paris, Warsaw, Geneva, Belfast, San Juan, and Berlin; and Ben Shahn, a friend of Peter Blume, began painting his series of twenty-three starkly realistic works concerning the case, the most representative being *The Passion of Sacco and Vanzetti*, which depicts a judge and two other men staring blankly ahead and holding lilies over the open caskets of the two Italian anarchists. A group of intellectuals, including Margaret Wilson, daughter of Woodrow Wilson, Susan Glaspell, Frank Shay, and Mona T. Cheney, sent a petition to Governor Fuller asking him to prevent the "legalized lynching."

In August 1927, Millay became actively involved in the

Sacco-Vanzetti trial. On August 20, Boston sympathizers sent out an appeal for picketers to which Millay responded. During the next two days, thousands of picketers appeared in Boston. Millay and John Dos Passos led a separate demonstration on August 22, for which they were promptly arrested, and Eugen came to the Joy Street Station and bailed Millay out of jail. On August 22, Millay's poem "Justice Denied in Massachusetts" was printed in the New York *Times*. That afternoon she had an audience with Governor Fuller, whom she urged to grant clemency to the two men. That night Millay composed an impassioned letter to Governor Fuller, which concluded:

> You promised me, and I believed you truly, that you would think of what I said. I exact of you this promise now. Be for a moment alone with yourself. Let fall from your harassed mind all, all save this: which way would He have turned, this Jesus of your faith?

> I cry to you with a million voices: answer our doubt. Exert the clemency which your high office affords.

> There is need in Massachusetts of a great man tonight. It is not yet too late for you to be that man.

Sacco and Vanzetti were executed a few minutes after midnight on August 23. That afternoon Millay was found guilty of picketing, but she appealed and was acquitted on December 3, 1927.

Impassioned by the injustice to Sacco and Vanzetti, whose names have not been cleared even today, Millay wrote several poems berating their oppressors—"Justice Denied in Massachusetts," "The Anguish," "Hangman's Oak," and "Wine From These Grapes." "Justice Denied in Massachusetts" contains images of the blighted crops, the ruined traditions of justice and free speech, beneath the cloud of injustice in Massachusetts:

> Shall the larkspur blossom or the corn grow under this cloud?
> Sour to the fruitful seed
> Is the cold earth under this cloud,

> Fostering quack and weed, we have marched upon
>   but cannot conquer....

Famine creeps over the land as the hayrack is deserted, petals drop to the ground, trees bear no fruit, the sun does not shine, crops do not grow, and slugs and mildew plunder the larkspur and corn. In the first stanza, Millay chides New Englanders for their supposed indifference to the fate of the Italian anarchists:

> Let us abandon then our gardens and go home
> And sit in the sitting-room.

By the last stanza, Millay expresses deep bitterness and a sense of loss over a government that denies freedom of speech, belief, and action:

> Let us sit here, sit still,
> Here in the sitting-room until we die;
> At the step of Death on the walk, rise and go;
> Leaving to our children's children this beautiful door-
>   way,
> And this elm,
> And a blighted earth to till
> With a broken hoe.

Although Millay's use of vegetation imagery gives the poem some aesthetic distance, the separation between the author and her work, the poem still is heavy with didacticism, such as "We have marched upon but cannot conquer..." and "We shall die in darkness, and be buried in the rain."

Both "Hangman's Oak" and "The Anguish" contain even more propaganda than "Justice Denied in Massachusetts." Comparing the execution of Sacco and Vanzetti to an old west lynching, Millay concludes,

> Side by side together in the belly of Death
>   We sit without hope,
> You, and I, and the mother that gave you breath,
>   And the tree, and the rope.

"The Anguish" capsules a feeling of cosmic pain, comparable to Christ's passion on the cross:

The anguish of the world is on my tongue.
My bowl is filled to the brim with it; there is more
    than I can eat.
Happy are the toothless old and the toothless young,
That cannot rend this meat.

Regardless of how sincere Millay was in her social concern, she sacrificed finely chiseled art for inferior journalism. As Harriet Monroe astutely remarked, "The Sacco-Vanzetti case stirred her, but it did not quite possess her; the poems it gave her were relatively unspontaneous and heavy."[34]

Several years after the travesty of Sacco and Vanzetti, Millay expanded her social consciousness to include a concern with communism. In 1936, Millay completed the manuscript of *Conversation at Midnight*, which is basically a philosophical treatise on the relative merits of capitalism and communism, though other topics are explored. The seven main characters represent various classes of society: Merton, a distinguished stockbroker; Carl, a communist poet; Pygmalion, a disillusioned playwright; Father Anselmo, a Roman Catholic priest; Ricardo (the host), a wealthy, liberal agnostic; Lucas, a young, idealistic advertising writer; and John, a religious painter. Throughout the dialogue, the men simply exchange points of view without reaching any conclusions. Merton tells Carl, "Your masses are fleas, not men...." In defense of communism, Carl utters the only real poetry in *Conversation*:

Life itself is a weed by the roadside, a common, golden weed.
Give us back the eyes of our childhood, freed
From the squint of appraisal, the horny glint of greed!

Beautiful as a dandelion-blossom, golden in the green grass,
This life can be.
Common as a dandelion-blossom, beautiful in the clean grass,
    not beautiful
Because common, beautiful because beautiful;
Noble because common, because free.

Pygmalion exclaims, "The world stinks. It stinks like a dead cat under a door- / step. It stinks to hell." A sharp departure from Millay's earlier spontaneous work, "*Conversation* comes mainly from the head and not the heart."[35] As Millay's social consciousness grew, she reversed her antiwar position as expressed in *Aria da Capo*. Impassioned by the conviction that America should enter World War II, Millay hastily wrote *Make Bright the Arrows* in 1940. Fully aware of the work's artistic inferiority, Millay wrote Charlotte Babcock Sills, "I have one thing to give in the service of my country,—my reputation as a poet." Even knowing that *Make Bright the Arrows* is pure propaganda, one is amazed to discover that Millay was capable of writing so terribly as the title poem suggests:

> Make bright the arrows,
>   Gather the shields:
> Conquest narrows
>   The peaceful fields.
>
> Stock well the quiver
>   With arrows bright:
> The bowman feared
>   Need never fight.
>
> Make bright the arrows,
>   O peaceful and wise!
> Gather the shields
>   Against surprise.

The poems in this volume are repetitive, formless, didactic, and mundane.

Part of Millay's passion over World War II stemmed from a concern about Eugen's family, which was still in Holland. Two of the poems in *Arrows* deal specifically with the Netherlands. "I Forgot for a Moment" refers to tulips, lowlands, canals, and ships, and "I Dreamt the Lowlands" treats three dykes, the Watcher, the Dreamer, and the Sleeper, that protect a stretch of Dutch coastland from the North Sea.

Edmund Wilson wrote of *Make Bright the Arrows*:

> I was confirmed in my supposition that these poems had been
> inspired by loyalty to Eugen....One of his cousins had been tor-
> tured and killed; others had had hairbreath escapes. Edna now
> constantly sent them packages. She always spoke of "our rela-
> tives," and one could see that she was very much attached to
> them. She had visited them in Holland and had even learned the
> language.[36]

Millay continued to write propaganda in "Poem and Prayer
for an Invading Army" (1944) and "For my Brother Han and
My Sisters, in Holland" (1945), a direct reference to the
Boissevain family.

After her marriage to Eugen Boissevain, Millay gradually
ceased to be the intensely personal poet of the Village and
took on the world, rather than her heart and mind, as her
province. Intellectually, Millay was quite capable of understanding world events, as her brilliant record in languages and
literature at Vassar and her powerful memory proved. Emotionally, however, she was better suited to deal with universal
problems of love, life, and death than with political issues, as
John H. Preston explains:

> The only real originality possible to man consists in setting down
> one's own individual impressions and emotions, the whole matter
> lying in the potential expansiveness of one's soul.

Love was Millay's religion. Ironically, the most universal
truths are the most personal, and love is one of the most self-
ish passions.[37] Thus, in becoming a spokesman for the world,
Millay no longer conversed with the universe. Perhaps Eugen
Boissevain was not solely to blame for Millay's propaganda
poetry. But there was a basic difference in Millay's reaction
to her husband and to her other Village suitors: Millay forced
Dell, Wilson, and Ficke to become aspects of her own personality, but she allowed herself to become a facet of Eugen's
personality.

Although Eugen Boissevain allowed Millay to become too

dependent on him, he was nevertheless a sorce of emotional stability for her. In Eugen, Millay found a man who respected her privacy, admired her work, nursed her through painful illnesses, and fully accepted her as a poet, woman, and fellow human being.

Both Edmund Wilson and Elizabeth Atkins felt that Millay wrote *Fatal Interview* to one of her lovers outside her marriage. But one of these sonnets, "Love is not all," seems the perfect expression of Millay's sentiments about her husband, to whom she had been married for eight years when she wrote the poem and who had taught her the beauty of enduring love. The first four lines of the octave strongly suggest sexual love:

> Love is not all: it is not meat nor drink
> Nor slumber nor a roof against the rain;
> Nor yet a floating spar to men that sink
> And rise and sink and rise and sink again....

In the second half of the octave, Millay contrasts love with physical illness, a possible reference to Eugen's care for her during her illnesses:

> Love can not fill the thickened lung with breath,
> Nor clean the blood, nor set the fractured bone;
> Yet many a man is making friends with death
> Even as I speak, for lack of love alone.

In the sestet of the sonnet, Millay expresses her love for Boissevain—"husband, lover, and the best friend she ever had"—in the most human terms:

> It may well be that in a difficult hour,
> Pinned down by pain and moaning for release,
> Or nagged by want past resolution's power,
> I might be driven to sell your love for peace,
> Or trade the memory of this night for food.
> It well may be. I do not think I would.

8

Summary

As the hours of October 18, 1950, wore away, Edna St. Vincent Millay sat up through the night, sustained by coffee and cigarettes, reading the proofs of Rolfe Humphries' translation of the *Aeneid*. Just before dawn, she poured herself a glass of Alsatian wine and started to walk upstairs. Feeling faint, she sat down on the first step above the landing at Steepletop. With a page of poetry in one hand and a glass of wine in the other, Edna Millay died quietly of a heart attack.[1]

Many years before, Greenwich Village had served as both the backdrop and the catalyst for an important transformation in the life and works of Edna St. Vincent Millay. What Lambert Strether found in Paris—"those spontaneous joys that come from the contemplation of beauty, the culture of the mind and uncalculating love for a fellow creature"[2]—is not so different from what Millay discovered in New York. Away from her "pink-and-gray college," Millay found new, exciting people and ideas in the Village. Although she was unimpressed by cubism, Freudianism, imagism, and political activism, she developed a Whitmanesque love for the common man, which the Ash Can School depicted, and a strong belief in the right of women to become real individuals.

During the Pre-Twenties, the Village was a mecca for writers and artists—Floyd Dell, Edmund Wilson, Arthur Davison Ficke, Witter Bynner, John Reed, Max Eastman, Jig Cook, Susan Glaspell, Alfred Kreymborg, John Peale Bishop, Norma Millay, Charles Ellis, Malcolm Cowley, Kenneth Burke, Wallace Stevens, Theodore Dreiser, Eugene O'Neill, John Sloan, Robert Henri, and Peter Blume. Millay's particular coterie exerted a strong influence on her life and works.

Floyd Dell's greatest contribution to Millay was to help her clarify her attitude toward women. In *The Lamp and the Bell* (1921), clearly based on her Vassar days, Millay suggests that lesbian love is stronger than heterosexual love. Two years after she met Dell, however, Millay wrote the brilliant series of *Twenty Sonnets*, which were published in *Reedy's Mirror*. Several of these sonnets affirm the depth of love between a man and woman—"Into the golden vessel of great song," "I pray you if you love me, bear my joy," and "And you as well must die, beloved dust." Dell's supposed atheism perhaps led Millay to examine her orthodox views of religion, but she retained her deep love of the common man. As a socialist, pacifist, and revoluntionary, Dell possibly planted the seeds of social consciousness that ripened later in Millay's mind.

Edmund Wilson, who later became an outstanding twentieth-century critic, offered Millay a relationship that was a rare blend of the emotional and intellectual. Unlike Floyd Dell, Wilson was not given to meddling in Millay's innermost thoughts, although he was protective when she needed support. He introduced her to new cultural horizons in New York—opera, ballet, plays—as well as providing her with a much needed market for her poetry in *Vanity Fair*, of which he was an editor. Millay commemorated the intellectual aspect of their relationship in "Portrait," and Wilson illustrated the depth of their spiritual bond by his almost supernatural dream about her the night after her death.

A poet, lawyer, and art critic, Arthur Davison Ficke entered Millay's life nearly six years before her Village days with a letter congratulating her on her astounding poem "Renascence." When she finally met Ficke in February 1918, she again found a relationship based on both the emotional and the intellectual. After Ficke's three-day leave ended, Millay wrote him love letters and sonnets, including "There is no shelter in you anywhere," "Into the golden vessel of great song," and "And you as well must die, beloved dust." Millay greatly respected Ficke's critical abilities: shortly after her Village days, she asked him to help her completely revise her libretto *The King's Henchman*. Perhaps Ficke's romantic inaccessibility caused Millay to intensify her emotions about him in order to write more vivid poetry. But in Ficke, Millay first realized the possibility of permanent love, a sharp departure from her earlier view of love as transient.

In 1923, Millay married Eugen Boissevain, an educated and once wealthy importer. During his first marriage to Inez Milholland, Boissevain had developed a profound respect for independent and intelligent women and a sense of social consciousness. After her marriage Millay fully realized the permanence of love, as typified by the sonnet "Love is not all," probably written to Boissevain. An unhappy result of this marriage was a decline in the quality of Millay's poetry. Her increasing activity in political affairs led her to write much inferior poetry, including "Justice Denied in Massachusetts," "The Anguish," and "Hangman's Oak," all inspired by the Sacco-Vanzetti case, and *Make Bright the Arrows* and "Poem and Prayer for an Invading Army," which dealt with America's role in World War II. Although Eugen Boissevain was kind and strong person, he nevertheless allowed Millay to become too dependent on him and to view him as a father figure.

Several other Villagers contributed to Millay's growth as an artist and as a person. During her semester at Barnard College in 1913, Millay met Witter Bynner, a handsome, clever, and

subtly humorous poet and close friend of Arthur Davison
Ficke. For the rest of her life, Millay exchanged poems, criticism, and letters with Bynner. At one time, they were
engaged to be married but changed their plans, largely due to
the advice of Ficke.[3] In an article in the *New Republic*,
Bynner asserted that Millay was a finer poet than T. S. Eliot.[4]

Another of Millay's Village suitors, John Reed, was a
Marxist, adventurer, poet, and playwright. Due to his involvement with various causes—the Paterson strike, the Mexican
War, and the Russian Revolution—Reed allegedly did not
realize his full artistic potential.[5] They frequently engaged in
literary discussions; she explained the idea behind *Aria da
Capo* to him before she wrote the play.[6] After his death from
typhoid fever in the Russian Revolution and his subsequent
enshrinement as a martyr to the proletarian cause,[7] Millay
wrote to Reed the sonnet, "I see so clearly now my similar
years."[8] Her association with Malcolm Cowley, Kenneth
Burke, Alfred Kreymborg, Max Eastman and awareness of
the work of John Sloan also led to an awareness of new social
and artistic ideas.

Just as Floyd Dell became the representative man of the
Pre-Twenties, Edna Millay became the symbolic woman of
her era. To some, she became "the unrivaled embodiment of
sex appeal, the It-girl of the hour, the Miss America of
1920."[9] To others, she was a living symbol of freedom and
spontaneous joy. And to the postwar generation, she was
"not our conscience but our neurosis...."[10] The individual-
istic and egocentric young people of her era hailed her as
their poet because she was writing about them.[11] As "a
pagan with a troubled conscience and a peaceless heart,"[12]
Millay embodied the quest for new identity characteristic of
the Villagers and many young Americans. Moreover, "Miss
Millay would not have been heard had she not...moved to
Greenwich Village and made herself...the voice of a revolt in
life if not in letters."[13]

No doubt Millay's public image as an It-girl was largely created by the flippant poems in *A Few Figs from Thistles*, such as "First Fig," "Second Fig," "Recuerdo," "The Singing-Woman from the Wood's Edge," "Thursday," and the sonnet "Oh, think not I am faithful to a vow!" In "Thursday" especially Millay taunts her lover with her ideas of free love:

> And if I loved you Wednesday,
> > Well, what is that to you?
> I do not love you Thursday—
> > So much is true.
>
> And why you come complaining
> > Is more than I can see.
> I loved you Wednesday,—yes—but what
> > Is that to me?

The "lovers and thinkers" in Greenwich Village significantly altered the life and works of Edna St. Vincent Millay. Not only did she crystallize her concept of women's rights and develop a deep love for mankind, she also sharpened her "tough intellectual side" as she made her associates facets of her own imagination and treated love and loneliness with controlled objectivity. Max Eastman especially admired her courage, which he celebrated in a sonnet to Millay that concludes,

> Above the clash of battle, and the rage
> Which is existence in this place and age,
> Above all wounds and weapons it could send,
> You have held high and beautifully strong,
> And flowing rose-and-silver in the wind,
> The bold clear slender pennant of your song.[14]

Millay's Village poetry (*Renascence, A Few Figs from Thistles,* and *Second April*), and poetry clearly inspired by the Village (*The Harp-Weaver* and *The Buck in the Snow*), is her finest poetry. Perhaps she would not have written propaganda had she married some other of her Village suitors. Con-

jecture aside, however, the first five volumes of her poetry do
attest to the enormous impact of the "lovers and thinkers" in
the Village.

What Edna St. Vincent Millay gained from the Village was
the quality of courage—the courage to live spontaneously, to
love deeply, to feel grief and loneliness unashamedly, to defy
death. She died with a glass of wine in one hand and a page
of poetry in the other.

> Lovers and thinkers, into the earth with you.
> Be one with the dull, the indiscriminate dust.
> A fragment of what you felt, of what you knew,
> A formula, a phrase remains,—but the best is lost.
>
> Down, down, down into the darkness of the grave
> Gently they go, the beautiful, the tender, the kind;
> Quietly they go, the intelligent, the witty, the brave.
> I know. But I do not approve. And I am not resigned.

Notes

Chapter 1

1. Floyd Dell, *Homecoming: An Autobiography* (New York: Farrar and Rinehart Co., 1933), p. 306.

2. Norman Brittin suggests this four-part division of "Renascence." Norman Brittin, *Edna St. Vincent Millay* (New York: Twayne Publishers, 1967), pp. 70-71.

3. Miriam Gurko, *Restless Spirit: The Life of Edna St. Vincent Millay* (New York: Thomas Y. Crowell Co., 1962), p. 18.

4. Gladys Brown Ficke to the author, April 14, 1971.

5. Edwin Marion Cox, *The Poems of Sappho* (New York: Charles Scribner's Sons, 1925), pp. 14-15.

6. Edna St. Vincent Millay to Charlotte Babcock Sills, Oct. 12, 1919, Vassar Collection.

7. Mary McCarthy to the author, Nov. 1, 1970.

8. Henry Noble MacCracken, *The Hickory Limb* (New York: Charles Scribner's Sons, 1950), pp. 81, 157.

9. Brittin, *Millay*, p. 106.

10. Edna St. Vincent Millay, *Letters*, ed. Allan Ross Macdougall (New York: Grosset & Dunlap, 1952), p. 87.

11. *Letters*, p. 311.

Chapter 2

1. Interview with Greg Garcia, bartender, Chumley's Bar, New York, New York, Aug. 27, 1969.

2. Norma Millay Ellis to the author, Aug. 10, 1970.

3. Malcolm Cowley dismisses this statement as apocryphal.

4. Floyd Dell, *Love in Greenwich Village* (New York: George H. Doran, 1926), p. 15.

5. Caroline Ware, *Greenwich Village 1920-1930* (Cambridge, Mass.: The Riverside Press, 1935), p. 10.

6. Hereafter the term Pre-Twenties refers to the decade 1910 to 1920.

7. Interview with Gladys Brown Ficke, Hotel Sarasota, Sarasota, Florida, Feb. 5, 1971.

8. Dell, *Homecoming*, pp. 246-47.

9. Ware, p. 53.

10. Dell, *Homecoming* p. 257.

11. Barbara Rose, *American Art Since 1900: A Critical History* (New York: Frederick Praeger, 1967), pp. 70-71.

12. *Letters*, pp. 35-36.

13. Rose, p. 129.

14. Harriet Monroe, *A Poet's Life: Seventy Years in a Changing World* (New York: The MacMillan Co., 1938), pp. 406-07.

15. Malcolm Cowley, rev. of *The Poet and Her Book: A Biography of Edna St. Vincent Millay*, by Jean Gould, *Book World*, May 13, 1969, p. 5.

16. Interview with Malcolm Cowley, Hollins College, Hollins, Virginia, March 30, 1970.

17. Interview with Norma Millay Ellis, Steepletop, Austerlitz, New York, Aug. 21, 1970.

18. Malcolm Cowley interview.

19. For more information on Millay's Nancy Boyd articles, see Norman Brittin's "Edna St. Vincent Millay's 'Nancy Boyd' Stories," *Ball State University Forum*, 10, No. 2 (Spring 1969), 31-36.

20. Several critics, including Norman Brittin, believe that "Recuerdo" was written about Salomon de la Selva. I think Floyd Dell was the man involved because the poem was published *after* she met Dell.

Chapter 3

1. Dell, *Homecoming*, p. 309.

2. Floyd Dell, *Moon-Calf: A Novel* (New York: Alfred A. Knopf, 1921), p. 350.

3. Dell, *Homecoming*, p. 291.

4. Cowley, rev. of *The Poet and Her Book*, p. 5.

5. Dell, *Love*, pp. 32-33; Dell, *Homecoming*, p. 299.

6. Jean Gould, *The Poet and Her Book: A Life of Edna St. Vincent*

Millay (New York: Dodd, Mead and Co., 1969), pp. 83-84.

7. Dell, *Homecoming*, p. 301.

8. Monroe, *Poet's Life*, p. 310.

9. Edna St. Vincent Millay to Mr. Moe, March 10, 1933, property of Newberry Library.

10. Dell, *Homecoming*, p. 26.

11. *Letters*, p. 104.

12. Dell, *Homecoming* pp. 304-07.

13. Floyd Dell interview with Norman Brittin, property of Norman Brittin.

14. Brittin, *Millay*, p. 102.

15. Gurko, p. 106.

Chapter 4

1. Edmund Wilson, *I Thought of Daisy* (Baltimore, Md.: Penguin Books, 1929), pp. 29-34.

2. Edmund Wilson, *The Shores of Light: A Literary Chronicle of the Twenties and Thirties* (New York: Random House, 1952), p. 751.

3. *Letters*, pp. 105-06.

4. *Letters*, pp. 159-60.

5. *Letters*, pp. 173-74.

6. Wilson, *The Shores of Light*, p. 752.

7. Wilson, *The Shores of Light*, p. 764.

8. *Letters*, p. 153.

9. Wilson, *The Shores of Light*, p. 26.

10. Andrew Turnbull, *Scott Fitzgerald* (New York: Charles Scribner's Sons, 1962), pp. 58-59.

11. Turnbull, p. 121.

12. Edmund Wilson, *A Prelude: Landscapes, Characters, and Conversations from the Earlier Years of My Life* (New York: Farrar, Straus, and Giroux, 1967), p. 28.

13. Turnbull, p. 74.

14. Wilson, *Daisy*, p. 34.

15. Malcolm Cowley interview.

16. Wilson, *The Shores of Light*, p. 761.

17. Sherman Paul, *Edmund Wilson: A Study of Literary Vocation in Our Time* (Urbana, Ill.: Univ. of Illinois Press, 1965), p. 152.

18. Paul, p. 152.

19. Wilson, *The Shores of Light*, p. 773.

20. *Letters*, p. 334.

21. Wilson, *The Shores of Light*, p. 789.

Chapter 5

1. Dell, *Homecoming*, p. 307; Gurko, pp. 98-100; Brittin, *Millay*, p. 39.

2. *Letters*, p. 18-20.

3. *Letters*, p. 38.

4. *Letters*, p. 22.

5. *Letters*, p. 25.

6. *Letters*, p. 25.

7. *Letters*, p. 41.

8. Gladys Brown Ficke interview, Feb. 5, 1971.

9. Arthur Davison Ficke, "Arthur Davison Ficke," in *Twentieth Century Authors: A Biographical Dictionary of Modern Literature,* ed. Stanley T. Kunitz and Howard Haycroft (New York: The H. W. Wilson Co., 1942), p. 449.

10. Gladys Brown Ficke interview, Feb. 5, 1971.

11. Gladys Brown Ficke interview, Feb. 5, 1971.

12. Witter Bynner, "Ave Atque Vale," *Poetry*, 67 (April-Sept. 1946), 58.

13. Gladys Brown Ficke interview, Aug. 20, 1970.

14. Witter Bynner to Robert Farr, June 3, 1957, property of Norman A. Brittin.

15. *Letters*, p. 133.

16. *Letters*, p. 105.

17. Witter Bynner to Robert Farr, property of Norman A. Brittin.

18. Gladys Brown Ficke interview, Aug. 20, 1970.

19. *Letters*, p. 169.

20. Gladys Brown Ficke interview, Feb. 5, 1971.

21. Gladys Brown Ficke interview, Feb. 5, 1971.

22. Brittin, *Millay*, p. 40.

23. Ficke, "Preface: The Nature of Poetry," *Selected Poems* (New York: George H. Doran, 1926), p. v.

Chapter 6

1. *Letters*, p. 46.

2. Bynner, "Edna St. Vincent Millay," *New Republic*, 41 (Dec. 10, 1924), Winter Literary Section, 14-15.

3. *Letters*, p. 102.
4. *Letters*, p. 316.
5. *Letters*, pp. 102-03.
6. *Letters*, p. 139.
7. *Letters*, p. 141.
8. *Letters*, p. 169.
9. *Letters*, p. 146.
10. Gladys Brown Ficke interview, Feb. 5, 1971.
11. *Letters*, p. 258.
12. Brittin, *Millay*, p. 37.
13. Gurko, p. 105.
14. Brittin, *Millay*, p. 100.
15. Brittin, *Millay*, p. 116.
16. *Letters*, pp. 93-94.
17. *Letters*, p. 235.
18. *Letters*, p. 101.
19. W. Adolphe Roberts, "Tiger Lily," unpublished memoir, in Vassar Collection, pp. 3-4.
20. Roberts, pp. 5, 9.
21. Roberts, p. 16.
22. Wilson, *The Shores of Light*, pp. 751-55.
23. *Letters*, p. 209.
24. *Letters*, p. 340.
25. *Letters*, pp. 105-07.
26. Wilson, *The Shores of Light*, p. 751.
27. *Letters*, p. 340.
28. *Letters*, pp. 79-80.
29. *Letters*, pp. 119, 159, 213.
30. *Letters*, pp. 375-76.

Chapter 7

1. Gurko, pp. 154-55; Toby Shafter, *Edna St. Vincent Millay: America's Best-Loved Poet* (New York: Julian Messner, 1957), p. 147.
2. Eugen Boissevain, "Retired Importer," New York *Times*, Aug. 31, 1949, p. 23.
3. Gladys Brown Ficke interview, Aug. 20, 1970.
4. MacCracken, pp. 2, 25-26, 28.
5. Brittin, *Millay*, p. 53.
6. Gurko, p. 90.

7. Dell, *Homecoming*, p. 308.

8. Dell, *Homecoming*, p. 308.

9. Chicago *Times*, Aug. 5, 1923, p. 27.

10. Gladys Brown Ficke interview, Aug. 20, 1970.

11. *Letters*, p. 200.

12. Norma Millay Ellis interview.

13. Gladys Brown Ficke interview, Aug. 20, 1970.

14. Deems Taylor, "Edna St. Vincent Millay: 1892-1950," in *Commemorative Tributes of the American Academy of Arts and Letters 1942-1951*, p. 107, property of American Academy of Arts and Letters.

15. Allan Ross Macdougall, "Husband of a Genius," *Delineator*, 125 (Oct., 1934), 40-41.

16. Gladys Brown Ficke interview, Aug. 20, 1970.

17. Macdougall, 41.

18. Gurko, p. 168.

19. Witter Bynner to Robert Farr, property of Norman A. Brittin.

20. Witter Bynner to Norman A. Brittin, June 19, 1963, property of Norman A. Brittin.

21. Gladys Brown Ficke interview, Feb. 5, 1971.

22. Edna St. Vincent Millay to Witter Bynner, May 2, 1935, property of Harvard Univ.

23. Wilson, *The Shores of Light*, p. 777.

24. Gladys Brown Ficke interview, Aug. 20, 1970.

25. Wilson, *The Shores of Light*, p. 779.

26. Gladys Brown Ficke interview, Aug. 20, 1970.

27. Macdougall, pp. 29, 41.

28. Gladys Brown Ficke interview, Aug. 20, 1970.

29. Harrison Dowd interview with Norman A. Brittin, notes property of Norman A. Brittin.

30. Vincent Sheean, *Indigo Bunting: A Memoir of Edna St. Vincent Millay* (New York: Harper and Brothers, 1951), pp. 57-59.

31. Wilson, *The Shores of Light*, p. 784.

32. Macdougall, p. 41.

33. Brewster Ghiselen, "Introduction," *The Creative Process: A Symposium* (New York: New American Library, 1952), pp. 11-15.

34. Harriet Monroe, "Advance or Retreat?" *Poetry*, 38 (April-Sept. 1931), 219.

35. Brittin, *Millay*, p. 146.

36. Wilson, *The Shores of Light*, p. 785.

37. John H. Preston, "Edna St. Vincent Millay," *VQR*, 3 (1927), 343-48.

Chapter 8

1. Gurko, p. 256.

2. Joan Bennett, "The Art of Henry James: *The Ambassadors*," *Chicago Review*, 9, No. 4 (Winter 1956), 26.

3. Witter Bynner to Robert Farr, property of Norman A. Brittin.

4. Bynner, "Edna St. Vincent Millay," 15.

5. Dell, *Love*, pp. 27-28.

6. Brittin, *Millay*, p. 100.

7. Monroe, *Poet's Life*, p. 293.

8. Brittin, *Millay*, p. 113.

9. Elizabeth Atkins, *Edna St. Vincent Millay and Her Times* (New York: Russell and Russell, 1936), p. 70.

10. Bette Richart, "Edna St. Vincent Millay: Poet of Our Youth," *Commonweal*, 66 (1957), 150.

11. "The Literary Spotlight: Edna St. Vincent Millay," *Bookman*, 56, No. 3 (Nov. 1922), 274.

12. Ludwig Lewisohn, *Expression in America* (New York: Harper and Brothers, 1932), p. 576.

13. Lewisohn, p. 373.

14. Max Eastman, "A Passing Fashion," *Nation*, 127, No. 3309 (Dec. 5, 1928), 630.

Bibliography

Works by Edna St. Vincent Millay
POETRY

Renascence and Other Poems. New York: Mitchell Kennerly, 1917.

A Few Figs from Thistles. New York: Frank Shay, 1920.

Second April. New York: Mitchell Kennerly, 1921.

The Harp-Weaver and Other Poems. New York and London: Harper and Brothers, 1923.

The Buck in the Snow. New York and London: Harper and Brothers, 1928.

Poems Selected for Young People. New York and London: Harper and Brothers, 1929.

Fatal Interview. New York and London: Harper and Brothers, 1931.

Wine from These Grapes. New York and London: Harper and Brothers, 1934.

Huntsman, What Quarry? New York and London: Harper and Brothers, 1939.

Make Bright the Arrows, 1940 Notebook. New York and London: Harper and Brothers, 1940.

Invocation to the Muses. New York and London: Harper and Brothers, 1941.

Collected Sonnets. New York and London: Harper and Brothers, 1941.

Collected Lyrics. New York and London: Harper and Brothers, 1943.

"Poem and Prayer for an Invading Army." New York: National Broadcasting Co., 1944.

Mine the Harvest. New York and London: Harper and Brothers, 1954.

Collected Poems. New York: Harper and Brothers, 1956.

PLAYS

The Wall of Dominoes. *Vassar Miscellany*, May, 1917.

Aria da Capo. *Reedy's Mirror*, March 18, 1920; New York: Mitchell Kennerly, 1921.

The Lamp and the Bell. New York: Frank Shay, 1921.

Two Slatterns and a King. Cincinnati: Stewart Kidd, 1921.

The King's Henchman. New York and London: Harper and Brothers, 1927.

The Princess Marries the Page. New York and London: Harper and Brothers, 1932.

PROSE

Distressing Dialogues (under pseudonym Nancy Boyd). New York and London: Harper and Brothers, 1924.

Conversation at Midnight. New York and London: Harper and Brothers, 1937.

Letters of Edna St. Vincent Millay. Ed. Allan Ross Macdougall. New York and London: Harper and Brothers, 1952.

Biography and Criticism

BOOKS

Abrams, M. H. *The Mirror and the Lamp: Romantic Theory and the Critical Tradition.* New York: W. W. Norton and Co., 1953.

Aristotle. *The Ethics of Aristotle.* Ed. J. A. K. Thompson. Baltimore, Md.: Penguin Books, 1953.

Atkins, Elizabeth. *Edna St. Vincent Millay and Her Times.* New York: Russell and Russell, 1936.

Berthoff, Warner. *Edmund Wilson.* Minneapolis, Minn.: Univ. of Minnesota Press, 1968.

Bishop, John Peale. *Collected Essays.* Ed. Edmund Wilson. New York: Charles Scribner's Sons, 1948.

Bogan, Louise. *Achievement in American Poetry 1900-1950.* Chicago: Henry Regnery Co., 1951.

Brittin, Norman A. *Edna St. Vincent Millay.* New York: Twayne Publishers, 1967.

Cowley, Malcolm. *After the Genteel Tradition: American Writers 1910-1930.* Carbondale, Ill.: Southern Illinois Univ. Press, 1965.

——. *Exiles Return: A Literary Odyssey of the 1920's.* New York: The Viking Press, 1951.

Cox, Edwin Marion. *The Poems of Sappho*. New York: Charles Scribner's Sons, 1925.

Dell, Floyd. *Homecoming: An Autobiography*. New York: Farrar and Rinehart Co., 1933.

——. *Love in Greenwich Village*. New York: George H. Doran Co., 1926.

——. *Moon-Calf: A Novel*. New York: Alfred A. Knopf, 1921.

——. *Sweet-and-Twenty*. *Contemporary One-Act Plays of 1921 (American)*. Ed. Frank Shay. Cincinnati: Stewart Kidd Co., 1922.

Ficke, Arthur Davison. *Selected Poems*. New York: George H. Doran Co., 1926.

——. *Sonnets of a Portrait-Painter and Other Sonnets*. New York: Mitchell Kennerly, 1922.

Fletcher, Joseph. *Situation Ethics*. Philadelphia: Westminister Press, 1966.

Frank, Charles P. *Edmund Wilson*. New York: Twayne Publishers, 1970.

Gould, Jean. *The Poet and Her Book: A Biography of Edna St. Vincent Millay*. New York: Dodd, Mead, and Co., 1969.

Gray, James. *Edna St. Vincent Millay*. Minneapolis, Minn.: Univ. of Minnesota Press, 1967.

Gurko, Miriam. *Restless Spirit: The Life of Edna St. Vincent Millay*. New York: Thomas Y. Crowell Co., 1962.

Hamilton, Edith. *Mythology: Timeless Tales of Gods and Heroes*. New York: New American Library, 1940.

King, Grace Hamilton. "The Development of the Social Consciousness of Edna St. Vincent Millay." Diss. New York Univ., 1943.

Lewisohn, Ludwig. *Expression in America*. New York: Harper and Brothers, 1932.

McCarthy, Mary. *The Group*. New York: Random House, 1963.

——. *The Groves of Academe*. New York: New American Library, 1951.

MacCracken, Henry Noble. *The Hickory Limb*. New York: Charles Scribner's Sons, 1950.

Monroe, Harriet. *A Poet's Life: Seventy Years in a Changing World*. New York: The Macmillan Co., 1938.

——. *Poets and Their Art*. Freeport, N. Y.: Books for Libraries Press, 1932.

Paul, Sherman. *Edmund Wilson: A Study of Literary Vocation in Our Time.* Urbana, Ill.: Univ. of Illinois Press, 1965.

Petitt, Jean Morris. "Edna St. Vincent Millay: A Critical Study of Her Poetry in Its Social and Literary Milieu." Diss. Vanderbilt Univ., 1955.

Robinson, David M. *Sappho and Her Influence.* Boston: Marshall Jones Co., 1924.

Rogers, Carl. *On Becoming a Person: A Therapist's View of Psychotherapy.* Boston: Houghton Mifflin Co., 1961.

Rose, Barbara. *American Art Since 1900: A Critical History.* New York: Frederick Praeger, 1967.

Shafter, Toby. *Edna St. Vincent Millay: America's Best-Loved Poet.* New York: Julian Messner, 1957.

Sheean, Vincent. *Indigo Bunting: A Memoir of Edna St. Vincent Millay.* New York: Harper and Brothers, 1951.

Slote, Bernice, ed. *April Twilights (1903),* by Willa Cather. Lincoln, Neb.: Univ, of Nebraska Press, 1964.

Smith, William Jay. *The Spectra Hoax.* Middletown, Conn.: Wesleyan Univ. Press, 1961.

Turnbull, Andrew. *Scott Fitzgerald.* New York: Charles Scribner's Sons, 1962.

Ware, Caroline. *Greenwich Village 1920-1930.* Cambridge, Mass.: The Riverside Press, 1935.

Weigall, Arthur. *Sappho of Lesbos: Her Life and Times.* New York: Frederick A. Stokes and Co., 1932.

Wilson, Edmund. *Axel's Castle: A Study in the Imaginative Literature of 1870 to 1930.* New York: Charles Scribner's Sons, 1931.

——. *Five Plays.* New York: Farrar, Straus, and Young, 1954.

——. *I Thought of Daisy.* Baltimore, Md.: Penguin Books, 1929.

——. *Memoirs of Hecate County.* Garden City, N. Y.: Doubleday and Co., 1946.

——. *A Piece of My Mind: Reflections at Sixty.* New York: Farrar, Straus, and Cudahy, 1956.

——. *A Prelude: Landscapes, Characters, and Conversations from the Earlier Years of My Life.* New York: Farrar, Straus and Giroux, 1967.

——. *The Shores of Light: A Literary Chronicle of the Twenties and Thirties.* New York: Random House, 1952.

ARTICLES

Aldington, Richard, et al. "Preface." *Some Imagist Poets*. Boston: Houghton Mifflin Co., 1915. Pp. v-viii.

"Arthur Davison Ficke." *The National Cyclopaedia of American Biography*. New York: J. T. White & Co., 1949. XXV, 289-90.

Bennett, Joan. "The Art of Henry James: *The Ambassadors*." *Chicago Review*, 9, No. 4 (Winter 1956), 12-26.

Brittin, Norman A. "Edna St. Vincent Millay's 'Nancy Boyd' Stories." *Ball State University Forum*, 10, No. 2 (Spring 1969), 31-36.

Burton, Katherine. "Edna St. Vincent Millay." *Commonweal*, 27 (March 11, 1938), 544-45.

Bynner, Witter. "Ave Atque Vale." *Poetry*, 67 (April-Sept. 1946), 56-58.

——. "Edna St. Vincent Millay." *New Republic*, 41 (Dec. 10, 1924), Winter Literary Section, 14-15.

Chapin, Katherine G. "A Poet and Her Letters." *New Republic*, 124 (Dec. 8, 1952), 24-25.

Cheney, Billie Gunter. " 'Renascence' and Millay's Childhood." Paper read before the Worthwhile Study Club, Oneonta, Alabama, March 12, 1970.

Ciardi, John. "Edna St. Vincent Millay: A Figure of Passionate Living." *Saturday Review of Literature*, 20, No. 2 (Nov. 11, 1950), 8-9, 77.

Clemens, Cyril. "The Passing of Edna St. Vincent Millay." *Hobbies*, 55 (Dec. 1950), 140-41.

Colum, Mary M. "Edna Millay and Her Time." *New Republic*, 124 (March 12, 1951), 17-18.

Cook, Harold Lewis. "Edna St. Vincent Millay." *A Bibliography of the Works of Edna St. Vincent Millay*. Ed. Karl Yost. New York: Harper and Brothers, 1937. Pp. 2-55.

Cowley, Malcolm. Review of *The Poet and Her Book: A Biography of Edna St. Vincent Millay*, by Jean Gould. *Book World*, May 13, 1969, p. 5.

Dabbs, James McBride. "Edna St. Vincent Millay: Not Resigned." *SAQ*, 37 (Jan. 1938), 54-66.

Davison, Edward. "Edna St. Vincent Millay." *English Journal*, 16 (Nov. 1927), 671-82.

Dell, Floyd, "My Friend Edna St. Vincent Millay." *Mark Twain Journal*, 12, No. 2 (1964), 1-3.

Deutsch, Babette. "Yankee Prophetess." *Saturday Review of Literature*, 35 (Nov. 15, 1952), 26.

Dubois, Arthur E. "Edna St. Vincent Millay." *Sewanee Review*, 43 (Jan.-March 1935), 80-104.

Eastman, Max. "A Passing Fashion." *Nation*, 127, No. 3309 (Dec. 5, 1928), 628-30.

———. "The Sweet Disease of Otherness: Edna Vincent Millay and the Birds." *American Mercury*, 74 (May 1952), 107-09.

Ficke, Arthur Davison. "Arthur Davison Ficke." *Twentieth Century Authors: A Biographical Dictionary of Modern Literature*. Ed. Stanley J. Kunitz and Howard Haycroft. New York: The H. W. Wilson Co., 1942. Pp. 448-49.

Flanner, Hildegarde. "Two Poets: Jeffers and Millay." *After the Genteel Tradition: American Writers 1910-1930*. Ed. Malcolm Cowley. Carbondale, Ill.: Southern Illinois Univ. Press, 1965. Pp. 155-67.

"Great Poetess Dies at 58." *Life*, 29 (Oct. 30, 1950), 42.

Hay, Sara Henderson. "In Memoriam." *The Stone and the Shell*. Pittsburgh: Univ. of Pittsburgh Press, 1959. P. 37.

Humphries, Rolfe. "Edna St. Vincent Millay: 1892-1950." *Nation*, 171 (Dec. 30, 1950), 704.

———. "Miss Millay as Artist." *Nation*, 153 (Dec. 20, 1941), 644-45.

Jones, Llewelleyn. "The Younger Woman Poets." *English Journal*, 13 (May 1924), 301-10.

"The Literary Spotlight: Edna St. Vincent Millay." *Bookman,* 56, No. 3 (Nov. 1922), 272-78.

Macdougall, Allan Ross. "Husband of a Genius." *Delineator*, 125 (Oct. 1934), 29, 40-41.

"Miss Millay, Poet on a Farm." *House and Gardens*, 82 (Nov. 1942), 40-41.

Nicholl, Louise Townsend. "A Late, Rich Harvest of Edna Millay." *New York Herald Tribune Book Review*, May 23, 1954, p. 5.

"Obituary." *Time*, 56, No. 2 (Oct. 30, 1950), 89.

Orel, Harold. "Tarnished Arrow: The Last Phase of Edna St. Vincent Millay." *Kansas Magazine*, 1 (1960), 73-78.

Parks, Edd Winfield. "Edna St. Vincent Millay." *Sewanee Review*, 38 (1930), 42-49.

Preston, John H. "Edna St. Vincent Millay." *Virginia Quarterly Review*, 3 (July 1927), 342-55.

Ransom, John Crowe. "The Poet as Woman." *Southern Review*, 12 (Spring 1937), 783-806.

Rascoe, Burton. "Miss Millay." *Newsweek*, 13 (May 22, 1939), 40.

Richart, Bette. "Edna St. Vincent Millay: Poet of Our Youth." *Commonweal*, 66 (1957), 150-51.

Roberts, W. Adolphe. "Tiger Lily." Unpublished memoir, Vassar College Library Collection. Pp 3-4.

Taggard, Genevieve. "A Woman's Anatomy of Love." *New York Herald Tribune Book Review*, 7, No. 2 (April 19, 1931), 3.

Tate, Allen. "Miss Millay's Sonnets." *New Republic*, 66 (May 6, 1931), 335-36.

Untermeyer, Louis. "Song from Thistles." *Saturday Review of Literature*, 5 (Oct. 13, 1928), 209.

Van Doren, Carl. "Edna St. Vincent Millay: Singer." *Century Magazine*, 106 (June 1923), 311-16.

Van Doren, Mark. "Women of Wit." *Nation*, 113, No. 2938 (Oct. 26, 1928), 481-82.

Wilson, Edmund. "Epilogue, 1952: Edna St. Vincent Millay." *The Shores of Light: A Literary Chronicle of the Twenties and Thirties*. New York: Random House, 1952. Pp. 744-93.

——. "Prologue, 1952: Christian Gauss as a Teacher of Literature." *The Shores of Light: A Literary Chronicle of the Twenties and Thirties.* New York: Random House, 1952. Pp. 3-26.

"Witter Bynner." *Twentieth Century Authors: A Biographical Dictionary of Modern Literature*, Supplement. Ed. Stanley J. Kunitz and Vineta Colby. New York: The H. W. Wilson Co., 1955. P. 231.

BIBLIOGRAPHIES

Brenni, Vito J. and John E. James. "Edna St. Vincent Millay: Selected Criticism." *Bulletin of Bibliography*, 23 (May-Aug. 1962), 177-78.

Patton, John J. "A Comprehensive Bibliography of Criticism of Edna St. Vincent Millay." *Serif*, 5, No. 3 (Sept. 1968), 10-32.

Yost, Karl. *A Bibliography of the Works of Edna St. Vincent Millay.* New York: Harper and Brothers, 1937.

INTERVIEWS

Brittin, Norman A. Millay scholar. Auburn University. Auburn, Ala. Feb. 12, 1971.

Cowley, Malcolm. Noted scholar and friend of Millay. Hollins College. Hollins, Va. March 30, 1970.

Ellis, Norma Millay. Sister of Millay. Steepletop. Austerlitz, N. Y. Aug. 21, 1970.

Ficke, Gladys Brown. Mrs. Arthur Davison Ficke. Hillsdale, N. Y. Aug. 20, 1970.

———. Hotel Sarasota. Sarasota, Fla. Feb. 5, 1971.

Garcia, Greg. Bartender. Chumley's Bar. New York, N. Y. Aug. 27, 1969.

LeMoyne, Roy. Cousin of Arthur Davison Ficke. Tallahassee, Fla. May 8, 1971.

Index